'By attending closely to the goings-on in a single, iconic institution, Susan Ashley's rich and insightful analysis deftly reveals not only how cultural organisations are inevitably enmeshed in the wider world but also the exciting possibilities that new ways of conceiving of their publicness might hold for museums of all kinds as they seek to enhance their relevance and value in the twenty-first century.'

– Richard Sandell, *University of Leicester, UK*

'*A Museum in Public* is a compelling and critical portrait of the Royal Ontario Museum in Toronto, circa 2008, at the moment of its multi-million dollar renaissance, which included a spectacular architectural facelift and the promise of a global meeting ground, an agora for all. Combining institutional analysis with ethnographic fieldwork, Ashley shows how lofty rhetoric outpaced action, and corporate cultural norms infiltrated most areas of public service. *A Museum in Public* demonstrates the layers of analysis needed to see through the emperor's new clothes, and to understand the workings of privilege, even as it is democratized. The book also offers glimpses of ways in which publics (including museum employees) carve out spaces of sociability and freedom in the museum. This is a welcome contribution to museum studies, and to the ongoing study of Canada's largest museum.'

– Shelley Ruth Butler, *McGill Institute for the Study of Canada, McGill University, Montreal, Canada*

I0462036

A Museum in Public

A Museum in Public critically examines the idea of museums as institutions of the public sphere. Using as a case study the Royal Ontario Museum (ROM), Canada's largest museum, the book interrogates the public nature and political dynamics of the ROM as it completed a multi-million-dollar 'Renaissance' architectural project.

Employing an empirically engaged cultural analysis of how publicness was reflected in the ideas, attitudes and behaviours of management, staff, and visitors, the book builds upon an ethnographic description of four public interfaces of institutional operations: structuring, positioning, exhibiting, and interacting. Conceptualizing ROM's new nature as 'celebrity publicness': engagement as publicity and not politics, Ashley offers insights into how – and whether – museums like the ROM might achieve political publicness through transparent, open communicative action. As a whole, the book asks museum practitioners and scholars to seriously consider how the ideals of contact zone and engagement – with their real need for dissent, conflict, and alternative ways of thinking – can truly be made possible within an administrative setting.

A Museum in Public will be a unique resource for scholars and students around the world who are engaged with the ongoing process of democratization in museums. Its on-the-ground reporting on practical organizational issues, offered in a shorter more accessible format, will attract and provoke museum practitioners.

Susan L.T. Ashley is Senior Lecturer in Creative and Cultural Industries Management and AHRC Leadership Fellow in (Multi)Cultural Heritage at Northumbria University, Newcastle upon Tyne, UK. She is a cultural studies scholar interested in what, how, and why heritage knowledge is created, shaped, communicated, and consumed in the public sphere. Dr Ashley has published widely, including *Diverse Spaces: Identity, Heritage and Community in Canadian Public Culture* (2013). She has 20 years of experience with culture and heritage sites across Canada.

Museums in Focus
Series Editor: Kylie Message
The Australian National University, Australia

Committed to the articulation of big, even risky, ideas in small format publications, 'Museums in Focus' challenges authors and readers to experiment with, innovate, and press museums and the intellectual frameworks through which we view these. It offers a platform for approaches that radically rethink the relationships between cultural and intellectual dissent and crisis and debates about museums, politics and the broader public sphere.

'Museums in Focus' is motivated by the intellectual hypothesis that museums are not innately 'useful', safe' or even 'public' places, and that recalibrating our thinking about them might benefit from adopting a more radical and oppositional form of logic and approach. Examining this problem requires a level of comfort with (or at least tolerance of) the idea of crisis, dissent, protest and radical thinking, and authors might benefit from considering how cultural and intellectual crisis, regeneration and anxiety have been dealt with in other disciplines and contexts.

Interpreting Objects in the Hybrid Museum
Collections and Cultural Policy
Helena Robinson

Global Trends in Museum Diplomacy
Post-Guggenheim Developments
Natalia Grincheva

A Museum in Public
Revisioning Canada's Royal Ontario Museum
Susan L.T. Ashley

www.routledge.com/Museums-in-Focus/book-series/MIF

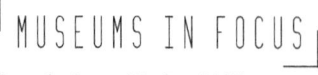

Logo by James Verdon (2017)

A Museum in Public
Revisioning Canada's Royal Ontario Museum

Susan L.T. Ashley

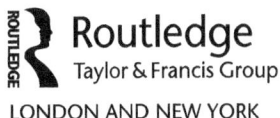
Routledge
Taylor & Francis Group

LONDON AND NEW YORK

First published 2020 by Routledge

2 Park Square, Milton Park, Abingdon, Oxon, OX14 4RN
605 Third Avenue, New York, NY 10017

Routledge is an imprint of the Taylor & Francis Group, an informa business

First issued in paperback 2020

British Library Cataloguing-in-Publication Data
A catalogue record for this book is available from the British
Library

Library of Congress Cataloging-in-Publication Data
A catalog record has been requested for this book

ISBN: 978-1-138-57926-2 (hbk)
ISBN: 978-0-367-78780-6 (pbk)

Typeset in Times New Roman
by Wearset Ltd, Boldon, Tyne and Wear

Contents

Part I
Setting the context

1   Boundary zone

The contrast was striking. I emerged from the hushed environment inside of one of Canada's largest museums, the Royal Ontario Museum, on a chilly day in January 2009 and met with a raucous wall of bodies hoisting placards and green, red and white flags. Young people mostly, in black and white chequered scarves, but a scattering of older folk as well. They were not looking back at the museum though; this crowd was decidedly fixated on the Israeli consulate across the street. ROM security guards patrolled the boundary between the protesters and the museum, keeping a pathway clear for visitors going in and out of the building.

Boundary zone not contact zone

Museum visitors were curious, not frightened. Some, like me, moved into the crowd and asked, 'what's going on?' Gaza protest. They snapped pictures. It was exciting. Demonstrators carrying flags of Lebanon and flags of Israel linked arms. Across the street a small throng behind a barrier shouted and gestured back at the protesters. An age-old quarrel.

I revelled in the exhilaration of the moment, that sense of being in the middle of something happening, something important because so many people were disturbed. And I wondered about the crazy juxtaposition here, not of warring activists from two sides of a long-standing conflict, but of this agitated public scene beside the cool, silent Crystal, the new museum building towering above. The square outside had become a public space for strident assembly although it had nothing to do with the museum. Why did this strike me as incongruous, or even ironic? The craggy architectural addition jutting out of the staid old museum exudes a sense of radical change; a collision of old and new (as often remarked by visitors), that should complement this kind of activist encounter. But instead I perceived a boundary between the institution and this kind of performance.

This is not to say that the Royal Ontario Museum (the ROM) had not proposed to be a place that could take on some of this excitement, activism, and change. This institution offered 'engagement' – but a genteel, polite, and managed engagement. I do not infer that museums must organize or host the kinds of democracy-in-action activities I witnessed on the ROM's doorstep. But I am asking, what does it take for the museum to truly live up to promises of engagement and act in ways that do not make me wonder at the incongruity of this scene? As impressive locations in the public sphere, as forms of media digested by mass publics, and as sites of government-funded public culture, why should I not expect and anticipate that this kind of performance would occur in the contact zone around the ROM? And how might a museum like the ROM react to and contribute to such enactments of public debate?

What intrigued me about this demonstration at its entrance doors was the relationship of this museum to public acts of politics. This was not the first time that social protests had engulfed the building. Located at the corner of two major streets in downtown Toronto, a scant 500 metres from the provincial legislature, the building has witnessed scores of political mobilizations, including the violent G20 repressions in June 2010 that had coincided with the opening ceremonies of the ROM's Terracotta Warriors blockbuster exhibition (another interesting juxtaposition). Despite its position as an institution devoted to producing and sharing knowledge, issues of power and politics rarely cross the border between those activities inside and outside the museum's walls.

The common thread that drew my attention outside the ROM the day of the Gaza protest was the *public* nature of this event: of this place, of this activity and its sensibility, and of the people who were present at the time. We were 'in public', on view, inhabiting public space, with a shared concern, situated next to a public institution with its own public role and public face – who drew a boundary between what it did and what the protesters were doing. But in addition, I was involved and complicit, on an even more personal level, with the publicness offered by the ROM within that boundary: I was a museum volunteer. I was in the museum, welcoming visitors on my bi-weekly shift, that day I encountered the Gaza protest outside. I was personally 'in public', on view, inhabiting public space, but in a vastly different manner. Thus, the nature of the museum's 'publicness' was even more striking to me, and appeared to be the right question to be discussing. The concept 'public' lies at the heart of democracy, where people come together to sort out matters of shared concern and must deal with both power and politics. From my embedded experience, the normative understanding of 'publicness' within museums like the ROM somehow avoids facing the political nature of the concept.

As a cultural studies scholar, I have been curious about how people participate and share in culture, particularly heritage-making practices, with culture and heritage writ large to include diverse activities from art exhibitions to quilting circles to protest marches. Relations and struggle over meaning-making are all central to cultural studies, involving power, control, and agency as well as sharing, community, and dialogue. Museums are situated as primary agents of meaning-making in the public sphere, in both their official capacity as quasi-governmental institutions and on an informal level as spaces for social interactions. I was interested in the ways that contemporary museums were attempting to reposition themselves in society as sites of meaning-making, seeking new roles, new audiences, and new activities. But in their search for new purpose, it seemed that the 'public' nature of their institutional role was in retreat. While 'public service' is well understood as the traditional mission of most museums, attitudes towards their publicness appear to have changed, challenged by state funding squeezes, shrinking government services, and the popularization and privatization of public culture. How do museums now view their public role, their public face, and their public responsibilities in relation to what goes on in the outside world? And what is the inherent politics in this work, which intervenes in human attitudes and relationships, and legitimizes particular ways of knowing?

A Museum in Public critically examines the assumptions that are made about the publicness of museum operations within one case study – the Royal Ontario Museum, Canada's largest museum. The book interrogates the public nature and political dynamics at the ROM as it carried out a complex revisioning of its public face: the multi-million-dollar Renaissance ROM (RenROM) project. The ROM is one of the few 'universal' museums in Canada, part of an international club of institutions like the British Museum and the Smithsonian Institution. During the RenROM project the museum was in a unique position of flux, transforming its architectural spaces and situating itself anew in relation to its globalizing context and community. In 2000, the ROM hired a new Director and CEO, William Thorsell, who came up with a dazzling plan to transform the museum, an architectural renaissance in the way the institution would show off its vast collections, but also transformational in the way it would solicit public engagement. That revitalization project was intended to show the museum as more dynamic, more relevant and, as one staff member remarked, 'a leading voice in the cultural life of the city' (Exhibit planner, 20 November 2009). The Governors' office enthusiastically described their Renaissance ROM project as one of the largest museum projects in the world and one of the most significant cultural projects in Canada.

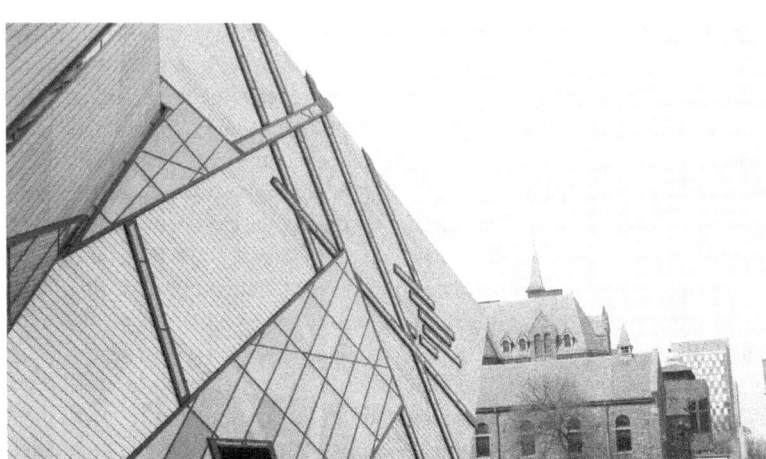

Figure 1.1 Royal Ontario Museum.
Source: photo courtesy of the author, Susan Ashley.

The Royal Ontario Museum was a 'public' institution, serving the public trust, and supported in part by allocations of provincial government monies of almost $28 million Cdn a year at the time of the research in 2009. It was obliged to account for its activities in public, transparent ways to the provincial government. It boasted over a million admissions of 'the public' every year; roughly half Canadians mostly from Toronto and southern Ontario (ROM Annual Report 2009). In addition to presenting itself 'in public' to these 'publics' through its stunning architectural presence at Bloor St. and Avenue Rd. in Toronto, the museum interacted with the world and exemplifies its public nature through a range of communicative means both on-site and externally. It presented permanent galleries and temporary exhibitions, hosted many thousands of school children, and offered tours, concerts, lectures, events, and a range of other programmes. It also positioned itself as a public agent through member services, volunteer programmes, research affiliations, media relations, marketing, international agreements, and other forms of corporate publicness.

I was interested in what, how, and why knowledge was created, shaped, represented, consumed, and debated publicly through the museum in this period, stressing the communicative nature of this process. The research employed an empirically and critically engaged analysis of the nature of the 'renaissance' that occurred at the ROM within the frame of the museum 'in public'. I studied how publicness was reflected in the attitudes and behaviours of management, staff, and visitors, building upon an ethnographic description of several facets of institutional operations. I demonstrate in the following pages how this museum's public function *was* transformed. Not only were the ROM's workers and managers redefining objectives and methodologies for this institution, but the museum was under unprecedented public scrutiny by governments, patrons, the media, audiences, and local residents. But while the renaissance project transformed the museum's physical character, the museum's new orientation towards public service called into question how it defined public value and served the public interest. It revealed the fundamental politics of power and status at work, where a publicness proposed as contact zone was hindered by acts of boundary-making.

Argued here is that the new public face of the ROM was a rhetorical one, a case of 'in public' celebrity that performed a reputation of relevance and engagement but did not manifest these qualities behind the scenes. While its corporate positioning spoke of public engagement and dialogue, its actions in practice demonstrated historical preoccupations of ownership and governance bound to property and status. Boundaries persisted between institutional interests and practices, and the lives and concerns of people for whom this public museum existed. This divide was the very essence of an 'in public' style of publicness: engagement as publicity not politics. This book contends that removing the boundaries between words and deeds, and between inside and out, is the essence of true publicness in its richest sense of bridging, dialogue, and democratic encounter. It offers insights into how – and whether – museums like the ROM might achieve political publicness through transparent, open and democratic communicative action. Such a process required significant organizational change, with removal of boundaries between rhetoric and deeds, management and workers, and inside and outside the museum.

Framing this study of museums and publicness

Publicness and the public sphere have been a focus of attention for political, communication, social, and cultural studies theorists. Publicness is defined here as 'The quality, condition, or fact of being public'; 'concerning the people' and/or 'being open to view' (Oxford English Dictionary). The publicness of museums is studied here from a cultural and communications disciplinary perspective, as a quality that relates to transparency: performances 'in public' can reveal workings of power within motivations, assumptions, and purposes. *A Museum in Public* takes an interdisciplinary perspective on museums as complex media forms communicating symbolic or expressive or meaning-making aspects of social behaviour, on both formal and informal levels. How cultural and social relationships were publicly expressed and negotiated are explored. The nature of these communicative relations has a unique character when enacted 'in public', and a museum's organization, in process and structure, can affect this quality in many ways. Important to the study was the cultural product (the museum space and organizational structures), the discursive practices (conditions and relations within its production and reception) and the larger sociocultural, economic, and governmental context and processes within which museums like the ROM are situated.

Museum studies is an interdisciplinary field that Kylie Message has called disciplinary 'borderwork' (Message 2009: 126), which she links to the persistent metaphor invoked by James Clifford (1997) that characterizes the museum as a 'contact zone'. Message argues that scholarly inquiry and debate about museums involves a mediation, transaction, or translation across disciplinary and cultural divides, and invokes both the separation and bringing together of ideas and people in creative juxtaposition. From an interdisciplinary perspective, social, communicative, and cultural processes within museums and the interrelationship of structures, policies, and meanings are all critical to understanding the institution's public nature. Thus my inquiry into the public nature of museums brings into play the boundaries and contact zones of museum studies, as well as the perspectives of communication and cultural studies.

My interest in public culture and communication in museums can also be characterized as critical social science. Bourdieu's concept of cultural 'field' within which social practices are shaped and reproduced through the interactions of various different and unequal agents has shaped this research (Bourdieu 1993). By studying the field, the interrelationship of both objective activities and use of power, and the aspirations, expectations, and actions of people are revealed. 'Critical museology', which has its origins in the new museology movement, also inspects power relationships. Andrew Dewdney describes critical museology as 'the effort to change the practices of museums along the path of their "democratization", or, put another way, towards the realisation of the museum as fully public' (Dewdney 2008). Gray and McCall (2018) call for more research into the material processes of museum bureaucracies as a way of making sense of these questions of control, power and democratization within museums (2018: 128).

This book does this from within one museum organization in a crucial historical period of its existence, looking not just at documentary evidence and interviews with managers from a detached analytical perspective, but taking the subjective outlook of 'engaged scholarship' as an immersed practitioner, to reflect critically on the experience of the researcher in knowledge-making. My own critical cultural studies perspective implies the need to critique and transform social/cultural relations within the field by investigating underlying ideologies or assumptions, analysing processes and practices, and identifying actions to effect change. Further, my viewpoint as a critical practitioner frames how I draw insights as someone embedded in the field, and situates my conclusions as interventions both in theory and in practice.

Critical studies of museums in Canada

A Museum in Public is uniquely situated within the Canadian cultural policy and museum production context, offering an original commentary on capitalism and managerialism within public culture in Canada, as well as contributing to museum theory and practice internationally. Books on Canadian museums are relatively rare and tend towards historical or professional orientations. Interestingly, two leading international perspectives on museum organizations are led by Canadians. Robert Janes is a key critical voice of museum administration internationally, but with actual museum practitioners, the books of Gail and Barry Lord (Lord Cultural Resources) are influential.

The research underpinning this book was undertaken at a time when critical scholarship about museums in Canada was a largely unexplored field (Cheney 2002). Even since that time, assessing the public impact of museums has not been a prominent policy concern in Canada. Museum studies tend to be undertaken to improve the organization and management of museums, more so than how and why museums are organized and managed. Work such as Janes (2009, 2015), Gosselin and Livingstone (2016) and Butler and Lehrer (2016) have made inroads here. Research that has emerged from anthropology, history, and education have foci that reflect those disciplinary perspectives, more so than critical perspectives. Museums have been drawn into debates about identity in Canada, as part of discussions of representation and mediation of public history, and into cultural policy discussions, but only a few have been singled out for exclusive treatment, and usually in relation to key controversies (Livingstone 2016). Studies of Canadian museums as social institutions, with a focus on sociological, communications, or cultural studies perspectives are still infrequent, addressing issues of history, representation, and education (e.g. Ashley 2005; Gosselin and Livingstone 2016; McTavish 2013). Only a few authors have critically addressed the role of the museum in the public sphere in Canada (e.g. Janes 2009; Trofanenko 2014), and few explicitly theorize on the nature of their publicness (Sharma 2015). The Royal Ontario Museum has been the subject of critical study only in relation to the *Into the Heart of Africa* exhibit, with several articles and a book on that subject (Butler 1999; Mackey 1995; Tator *et al.* 1998). That there has not been subsequent published work on the ROM is surprising, considering the amount of international attention that exhibition received. As one of the largest public cultural development projects in Canada, the ROM should attract new cultural policy and cultural economy investigations. This book is in the vanguard of this anticipated research.

Within these theoretical and historical perspectives, *A Museum in Public* aims to seriously consider whether the ideals of 'contact zone' and 'engagement' – with their real need for dissent, conflict, and alternative ways of thinking – are practically possible within an administrative setting. It explores how the ROM, at a particular historical juncture in Canada, situated itself as a 'public' cultural institution, operating in the public interest. The volume addresses the underlying assumptions about publicness that were reflected in the formal and informal accounts of the ROM 'in public', that is, within four key areas of public interfaces during the Renaissance ROM project. Questioned is the extent to which the museum served the public interest as a democratizing agent, and the factors that facilitated or hindered the application of this model. The book asks what insights might be drawn from the RenROM situation to inform whether the structure, processes, and practices of museums like the ROM could or should be reconfigured, so they might serve as agents of social change, inclusion, and negotiation.

Methodology

A Museum in Public reports on the ways that the idea of publicness was reconfigured during the Renaissance ROM period, and how it was reflected in the mission, organization, and activities of the museum – the research asks, *what does it mean for a museum to call itself a 'public' institution?* An awareness of the multifaceted, inconsistent, and negotiated nature of publicness underpins this inquiry. Reflexive, ethnographic research methods were used in order to assemble a picture of how the ROM as a case study defined itself as public, and perpetuated public processes within a changing social and economic context. Both texts and discourse were studied, a reflexive sociology approach that calls for a double analysis of social structures and practices from both an objective and a subjective point of view, allowing close inspection both of relations of power and relations of meaning about any phenomenon (Bourdieu and Wacquant 1992: 120–121). This meant undertaking not only the collection and analysis of objective data of policies, structures, and systems, but also a more subjective, taking-into-account of institutions as they exist in the minds of staff and visitors, and through their actual practices, using cultural, ethnographic tools. This dual approach implied a bridging to examine power structures *and* meaning-making, text, and discourse, on several levels within the institution. Reflexive sociology's two-stream analysis was most useful here because, what Public institutions do, and what they say they are going to do, are worth scrutinizing and are often different because of the rhetoric involved. The constitution of that public interface between rhetoric and actions was the focus of data collection. The ultimate aim was then to offer insights into the nature of the public interest that was served by the ROM and how that reflected a change in orientation, and to flag areas that might have relevance to museums more widely. The conclusions drawn from this research are not intended to provide broad generalizations of museum processes, but rather to offer a case study of a museum in a state of flux, a reflexive portrait within a critical perspective that casts light on how people and organizations make sense of their situations at the local level.

The most inhibiting limitation to this research was a problem of publicness: it quickly became evident that transparency, an aspect of publicness, would become an issue. Public access to detailed information, especially documentation, and access to people for interviews was difficult, or very slow. Certain departments seemed more eager to help the research than others. People lower in the hierarchy were most eager to voice conflicts with their senior managers. I could not know whether these transparency difficulties indicated internal dysfunction or absence of mind, or a desire to keep private certain information, or whether they indicated my own mistakes during initial interviews.

In this book

The following narrative first situates the many theoretical perspectives on publicness and the public as descriptive and existential qualities. It then introduces the museum and its RenROM project. Central chapters explore four public, communicative interfaces at the ROM during the revisioning project – Structuring, Positioning, Exhibiting, and Interacting. The chapters detail these facets of the ROM 'in public' through an objective and a subjective study of the museum's operations, examining power structures and meaning-making, texts and discourse. Each is situated as a unique organizational point of contact or boundary line reflecting the museum's public functions.

The final chapter wraps up the account of the competing politics and multiple, conflicting ideas about purpose, people, structures, and practices at the ROM. These remarks offer a personal intervention in both theory and practice: expanding both on theories of publicness and on the structures and practice of museum organizations. *A Museum in Public* argues that a clear understanding and application of the concept of 'publicness' is essential to open up the purpose and functioning of museums to democratic practices. Analysis of the institution's corporate positioning and relationships, its organizational structures, its exhibitionary and programming offerings, and its points of face-to-face interactions – all facets of the publicness that might have been subject to a renaissance – suggest that the museum at the time adopted new strategies, but not the kind of renaissance suggested by the museum's claims of change. The institutional face presented to the outside world through these interfaces involved 'publicity' at its most basic, with power and status invoked through each. The RenROM project as it was implemented did not resolve entrenched old-museum habits: wealthy patrons and privileged governing bodies, and old-fashioned exhibitionary and programming methods in its galleries. This apparent lack of change, despite Thorsell's words, revealed embedded attitudes towards the public role of the museum. As critics noted 'it is relatively easy to build or renovate' a museum, but any changes made in the redevelopment had little to do with 'the real issues confronting mainstream museums at a time of unprecedented societal change' (Janes 2010).

2 Publicness, public institutions, and the public interest

Understanding the role of the public sphere in society is central to the inquiry of this book and provides the conceptual focus where discussions of 'publicness', the public nature, or public purpose of museums can be situated. The museum profession consistently interprets the word 'public' as 'visitors', thus most debates about 'reinventing' museums flows from the need to understand their relationships with those people characterized as visitors or non-visitors (Anderson 2004). But museums are public in many senses of the word. They not only manage publics but are also spaces in the public realm that operate 'publicly'. The people who sit on museum Boards are not just members of the elite or stockholders of a business; they are representative of 'the public'. Museums are also: locations in the public sphere; serve publics often on behalf of public governments; protect and create 'public goods', and operate with a publicness that implies transparency and openness.

The term public, now associated with multiple definitions, has origins in the Latin publicus, meaning 'pertaining to the people'. As a noun, public can pertain to a physical location, and 'the public' can refer to 'the people' of a nation or some other community based on common interests (Dewey 1946 [1927]). Public as a noun might also refer to those things 'made' public, often represented or objectified through 'publicity', or as a verb, the action of making things public. As an adjective or adverb, it comes before another word and imbues it with meaning: such as accessible, visible, open, pertaining to government, or having to do with the populace as a whole (Newman and Clarke 2009). Nancy Fraser (1992) says the confusion or conflation of these different meanings of public has analytical, as well as political, consequences. For example, if an institution is funded privately, then it engenders different attitudes towards its function than if it was government or 'publicly' funded.

Public sphere

Current rethinking of the forms and practices of the 'public sphere' are especially relevant, as museums are framed as important locations in the public sphere (Barrett 2011; Hein 2006). The public sphere describes a discursive space for the exchange of reasoned opinions aimed at questions of collective concern (Habermas 1991). Habermas wrote of the emergence of the public sphere in eighteenth century European coffee houses and other bourgeois non-market and non-state locations, where private individuals came together for critical discussions about state power. Museums of that period have been proposed as one of those places where independent public opinion was formed, but whose later functional trajectory tended towards either commercialization or state/civic purposes (Bennett 2006: 49–50).

The debates on the nature of the public sphere generated by Habermas' foundational text contribute to theorizing the 'public' nature of museums and their communications. These address why and how publics come together to express, debate and negotiate relationships and common concerns (Sharma 2015). Normative accounts describe the public sphere as the foundation of democratic culture based on the principles of equality of participants, accessibility, and deliberation on the common good (Angus 2001; Calhoun 2005). This imbues much of the discourse around 'the' public sphere with a sense of civic morality: good public space is a sphere which is open and accessible to all, with social difference ignored (Iveson 1998). Before Habermas, Kant defined publicness as the 'transcendental concept of public right' based on citizens' fundamental dignity and moral sovereignty; as a moral principle and legal norm; and as an 'instrument' to achieve both individuals' independent reasoning and legal order in the social realm (Splichal 2006: 697).

But many scholars also point out that the public sphere in such a conception represented bourgeois or dominant interests as the universal norm, in opposition to others in society, particularly women and the working class (Fraser 1992). Michael Warner (2002) argued that there is no one single public sphere; they are always multiple, heterogeneous, competing, and unequal, with new groups continually being formed. Warner proposed the idea of '*counter*-publics' as sites autonomous or in opposition to institutional sites of dominant cultural players. Iveson (1998) described how certain public spheres (such as museums), which function as ceremonial sites of symbolic order, thus become targets for *dis*order by groups of people who themselves are denoted as 'counter-publics'. These ideas about publicness as a sphere for group interactions are all relevant to the functioning of museums as public.

The public and publics

Most museums think of the word public as *the* public, or those people outside who may visit a museum (Weil 1997). But the definition in this usage is far more complex than simply 'audience'. *The* public can be used to denote groups of people, often the generalized citizens of a nation, but also open-membership groups that coalesce around objects of interest, such as cultural forms, practices or institutions. A group of people is just a crowd until there is a focus, which then makes it a public – their formation requires interestedness or attention or address to some context (Warner 2002).

The public of cultural institutions has come to mean the 'audiences' for communications (Hannay 2005; Sharma 2015). The public, seen as a museum's audience, is then differentiated based on their interests: tourists, school children, social policy beneficiaries, artists and intellectuals, volunteers, and so on, which affects how communications are shaped. But the agency of the individuals, even when differentiated, is not admitted, that is, they are situated as receivers of information. When perceived as receivers of communication, the public sometimes takes on a sense of *mass*; it is undifferentiated and passive. It may also be ideal or symbolic, with members, meanings, values, and relationships chosen and frozen. This allows the massified public either to encompass all individualities – or to exclude some. Building an ideal or symbolic public is made possible through media publicity and cultural representations (Ku 2000).

John Dewey (1946 [1927]), a central theorist of publics, framed the public as active citizens who share in the effects of a political action, so have an interest in controlling those consequences. 'Publics' (with an 's') has been proposed as a broader formulation that invokes this agency on the part of group members, who tend to be loosely organized and egalitarian in their internal workings and membership (Simon and Ashley 2010). Any publics framed in terms of agency are dynamic and changing: they have different motivations, attitudes, and rules about membership. When publics are interpreted as active agents, they are framed as individuals, and actively enable participation or give voice, which entails sharing and belonging, but also negotiation and struggle (Bernard 1999).

One practical implication of such publics is that group members must deal with those with whom they do not or cannot identify. Calhoun wrote that such publicness is a process that is inherently about 'stranger sociability', where people who are not the same as each other connect, an effect amplified by media technologies (2005: 5). Arriving at this state involves complex factors and real tensions that arise when trying to simultaneously affirm and abolish differences (Fraser 2005). Iveson (1998) wrote that the creation of public spaces is sometimes mistakenly claimed to *generate* such community, that is, 'publics' of strangers. But he warned,

> whenever a public space is judged to be successful because a community of users has been established, we should be suspicious. In whose interests is such cultural homogeneity or integration established, and in whose image? Who are the outsiders that constitute the flip side of a community of insiders, and how can they be included if a good public space is one where everyone knows, or at least understands, each other?
>
> (Iveson 1998: 25)

Iveson describes those problems, inherent in museums' typical rhetoric about the way their activities generate publics defined, as a community of users. Publicness must instead be seen as more of a process, a coming together that transcends locations or sets of people, in a creative practice of *world-making* (Arendt 1998 [1958]). Publics formation involves the coming together of those strangers who are not massified, in ideal relationships of mutual understanding and positive reciprocity (Young 1990). In world-making, intersubjective discourses emerge from multiple, heterogeneous publics that create spaces in common. This brings to the fore 'the very idea of poiesis, understood as a creative doing; as action that carries the potential of something new, emergent, and not already predicted by a pre-existing form' (Simon and Ashley 2010: 251).

This kind of productive publicness lies at the foundation of democratic practice, of engagement in its ideal form – a form of publicness I experienced outside the ROM but one I needed to look at closely to find within. Some museum scholars have linked the increasing effects of new media forms in society to this kind of emergent sociality. But new media forms have generated effects that challenge traditional museum practices, such as the perceived decline of interest in embodied encounters with objects and people, a desire for more online experiences, and the demand for non-expert knowledge-building by publics within museum spaces (Cameron 2003, 2006).

The common good

Also assumed is that publics have shared concerns of a positive nature, associated with the concept of 'public interest' or 'public good', which denotes 'for the shared welfare' of the people. What constitutes those things that are good for the public, or in their interests, is highly contested. Calhoun (2005) considers 'the common good' to be foundational to democracy, based on the principles of equality of participants, accessibility, and deliberation. Habermas saw the need for benign, non-self-destructive 'communicative reasoning' that he felt emerged from public association and communication in a fair manner that is unencumbered by ideological orientations and strategic actions of commerce and power politics (Mackey 1995).

Current discussions of the public interest or common good of museums emphasize their role in organizing, preserving, and communicating perceptions and remnants of the past. 'Public memory' for example, is addressed as a public good; a collective past constituted through shared discourses and practices (Nora 1989). A shared history is perceived as crucial to the formation of the 'imagined community' or 'imagined nation', and through technologies like museums, people can imagine that they belong to this broader collective (Anderson 1983). Many foundational museum scholars have discussed, however, the way representations of public histories are more likely hegemonic tools employed by dominant institutions as part of the modernist project, by producing and reproducing certain types of knowledge and ways of knowing (e.g. Bennett 1995; Duncan 1995; Hooper-Greenhill 2003). Critics have thus called into question museums' particular 'public interest' as tools of the state rather than sources for democracy. Bennett (2006) critiqued the idea that museums could serve as public spheres in a democratic sense because they historically served as governmental apparatus for civic or national identity-building, social control or improvement, and economic development.

Also worth noting is the difficulty of the application of the democratic ideal of 'the common good' to real-world democratic processes where difference, disagreements, and compromise may have negative results. Bernadette Lynch (2017) has argued that museums must recognize their complicity in suppressing or anesthetizing social conflict in the ways they serve the public good. Public spaces and processes, Chantal Mouffe wrote, are 'agonistic' in that there will always be differences and antagonistic struggles that may not result in compromise and commonality (Mouffe 2000). This is an ongoing effect of 'making things public' that has erupted in museums in many instances (see Butler 1999; Dean 2009). The most prominent example in the Canadian context occurred at the ROM itself, when their *Into the Heart of Africa* exhibition was violently protested in 1989–1990. Here divergent perceptions of the 'public interest' of the museum were clear: the museum administration and curators, generally supported by the press, on one side arguing for academic freedom, and, a smaller 'counter-public' on the other denouncing racism, cultural insensitivity and white privilege (Tator *et al.* 1998).

Government as public

The idea of publicness being the creation and sharing of goods in common is invoked in another sense, that of Public (with a capital 'P') seen as pertaining to the state or governments. The word Public attached to any other word, like 'institution' implies government jurisdiction. Clearly museums in Canada are viewed as Public institutions because they tend to be owned or funded by governments. Through governments people share resources, services, and programmes that are designed to help citizens live together. On the flip side, however, Public seen as the state is associated with problems of coercion, inclusion/exclusion, bureaucracy, and professional power (Newman and Clarke 2009). The institutionalizing of Public in this way renders the nature of the publicness dull, habitual, and sedimented, losing an earlier dynamism inherent the process of *making things* public through enlarging and multiplying spheres and publics (ibid.; Latour 2005). The replacement of people acting in relation to each other, by institutions acting on their behalf, appears to be the case with museums – this is where history is 'kept'. It is habitually agreed that these public institutions represent the people and can speak for them in matters about cultural and natural heritage, and have become locations for accumulation of information, material and financial resources – 'Public' institutions.

Internationally, museological discourse around museums as governmental institutions in the public sphere has received robust attention, especially their historic role as hegemonic tools: categorizing knowledge, regulating visitors, and determining what themes and subjects may or may not be displayed and discussed (e.g. Bennett 1995; Hooper-Greenhill 2003). More recent discussions in museum studies have focused on museums as tools for government social cohesion and inclusion policies (e.g. Lynch 2017; Shiekh 2004) or as a utilitarian resource (Message 2007). In the UK, public 'engagement' and 'value' has been a research emphasis when culture as a resource became a priority public policy in the 2000s (e.g. Belfiore 2018; Dewdney 2008). In the US, 'civic engagement' has also become a prominent topic of museological research interest (Calhoun 2015; Weiser 2017). But such studies of museums and their social obligations still tend to be instrumental in their points of view. In dealing with such 'hot topics' museums tend to be risk-adverse (Cameron 2006).

In Canada, most museums operate as government or non-profit organizations, and 'Public' equates governmental/non-profit in public service on behalf of citizens. These institutions generally belong to the Canadian Museums Association (CMA), which defines its members as permanent, not-for-profit institutions whose exhibits are regularly open to the general public. CMA guidelines state on their website that 'Museums are institutions created in the public interest'. The CMA sets out what it calls the fundamental Public Trust responsibilities as public institutions: stewardship of collections and 'public service'. Public service is defined as the creation and advancement of knowledge and understanding, by making collections physically and intellectually available to all the communities served by the museum.

Public/private

Publicness has also come to mean the extent an organization is influenced by political authority, with 'privateness' constituted more positively as free from governmental authority. Neo-liberal attitudes and policies promote freedom from government interventions, and advocate the privatizing or individualizing of Public services (Giroux 2004; Robertson 2011). For some though, the loss of public space and services through private ownership is seen as an attack on democracy and opposed. Although privatized spheres of the marketplace, such as the agora, theatres, or shopping malls, appear to give some support and setting to 'public' life, there are always questions about ownership, and equality and fairness of access and voice. Calhoun believes this privatizing process underscores contemporary social change:

> Nothing is more basic to present day social change and social problems than unsettling of the relationship between public and private ... The issue is manifest when we speak of the public good vs. private goods, public finances vs. private property, public security and the surveillance of private life, or public culture, creativity and communication and the private control of knowledge as intellectual property rights. In all these arenas, and others, a tacit consensus about what is public and what is private has come unstuck.
>
> (2005: 1)

Museums have historically encouraged private sponsorship or sold various benefits to raise funds in order to survive economically (Abt 2006). In the nineteenth century, museum subjects and objects were gradually repositioned within commodity culture: Henning, referencing Bourdieu, has studied how the *pleasure* of collecting art for private use was transformed into the *use* of art for social appearances or conspicuous consumption (2006: 19). By the end of the twentieth century, large-scale museum redevelopments (for example the Musée d'Orsay in Paris or the Tate Modern in London) had become the technique of choice to boost civic tourism and urban redevelopment. The classic example is the Guggenheim Bilbao, a spectacular museum designed by architect Frank Gehry to transform the industrial city of Bilbao (Gray 2017).

Balancing the demands of private interests with public responsibilities has long been an uncomfortable act for most museum administrators. But some see this balancing act as tipping towards market orientations in sensibility and management style, which in turn influences how museums act on behalf of the public (Wu 2002). Under a corporatized and commoditized museum model, the 'public' is viewed as a consumer, public space becomes a commercial marketplace, and the public good resides in exchange value through manufactured pleasurable experiences (Janes 2009). Acts such as branding and naming of museum public spaces, and the franchising of museums such as the Guggenheim, are seen as clear demonstrations of the encroachment of 'private' values into institutions with 'public' responsibilities, and the museum operated as a site for consumption (Chong 2007; Message 2007). Such privatizing processes have begun to manifest at the Royal Ontario Museum.

Two other aspects of the public/private relationship are worth noting in relation to the ROM. Newman and Clark found that despite the apparent hegemony of market-populism discourses, citizens themselves still rate government public services as desirable and essential, and not replaceable by private services (2009: 178). Others have pointed out that private spaces can be claimed back for 'public' functions, that is, shared functions, from parades to protests to groups of young people using shopping malls to 'hang out' rather than for private consumption (Calhoun 2005; McLean 2012).

Presenting oneself 'in public' exposed to the public eye was an early function of European museums (Bennett 1995). Seeing and being seen was important to status ranking and social control. Early museums were among the first public spaces where women were allowed to be free from the private sphere of the home and in the public eye (Bailkin 2002). The display of 'private' or intimate goods, that is, objects of a sensitive nature that individuals or groups deem should not be seen 'in public', has also been raised as a moral issue in museums, for example some indigenous religious objects, and materials related to the Holocaust (Casey 2002; Ellsworth 2002). On the other hand, *exposure* to private details is sometimes valued in museums, as Bonnell and Simon noted, where difficult exhibitions with intimate details allow one to be 'open to the density of detail that traces another life' (2007: 69).

Openness

As noted above, visibility and openness are two characteristics inherent to a discussion of publicness. Being brought into the 'glare of publicity' is a metaphor that implies the exposure of ideas or activities to scrutiny for their truthfulness. Balancing the privateness required for decency or secrecy with the publicness required for honesty, credibility, and account-ability is a central ethical question in communication and political theory. What is public is what is visible, accessible or open to all – a quality that has sometimes been an object of struggle. Public credibility is an evalu-ative claim by citizens of the moral authority of actors, institutions, or whole governments on the basis of their publicness interpreted as openness (Ku 2000: 223). Crucially, keeping things private can also be seen as the process of hiding or obscuring things that should come into view. Lack of openness in the museum has been interpreted as ignoring histories, events or processes that constitute the narratives of society. In-visibility has been strongly criticized in relation to Black and minority presence within public histories in museums – not just kept private but written out entirely (Littler and Naidoo 2005).

Both visibility and openness are important public qualities for museums. But openness has been generally discussed more in terms of 'available to all', than as a political characteristic defining democratic practice. Openness of museum access has been criticized in terms of phys-ical entry and knowledge construction. Museum entrance fees have been one clear restriction on equal access. There has also been a lack of visibil-ity of behind-the-scenes knowledge production in museums, calling into question how contents and meaning are constructed (Hooper-Greenhill 2003). Institutional methods and professional practices have also been questioned because of inherent unequal power dynamics (Janes 2009). Museums have made efforts to locate and limit issues of power, for example repatriating cultural objects and opening up marginalizing narrat-ives through collaborations (Coombes and Phillips 2015; Peers and Brown 2003). However, such efforts tend to remain top-down in their decision-making and approaches, and actual openness or transparency has been dif-ficult (Lynch 2014).

New museology and publicness

Questions of the public role of museums and the nature of their publicness underscore theories in 'new museology'. New museology is a critical scholarship and practice that emerged in the 1970s, which critiqued mod-ernist institutional objectives and practices, and advocated that museums serve the public interest as agents of social life and change. Museologists at the time looked for ways to change radically the curator-dominated working methods, content, and structure of the institution. The purpose was to help museums achieve social relevance by contributing concretely to the conditions, interests and needs of the everyday lives of local populations, sometimes articulated as an ecology of relationships (Rivard 1985; Vergo 1989).

While the language of 'newness' has penetrated the mainstream in museum practice, how that has been interpreted differs widely. Some took up the idea that grassroots populations must play active roles in shaping the structure and organization of museums, which resulted in new institutional forms such as neighbourhood museums in the United States and ecomuseums in France and Quebec (Abram 2007; Rivard 1985). Newness has also been interpreted as intercultural exchange wherein the colonial practices of museums and their troubling relationships to 'Others' have been criticized and efforts made to alter practices (Boast 2011; Coombes and Phillips 2015). This questioning of the role and public nature of museums was led by ethnographers, who challenged the very business of representation and advocated a decentring of the museum towards a non-authoritative position as a community 'contact zone' accommodating meaning-making and dialogue among publics (Clifford 1997). These forms of new museology reflected Arendt's ideal of 'world-making' that results from publics forming in creative reciprocity.

But Message (2006a) pointed out a different interpretation of 'new' museology, in which modern museums rhetorically invoke newness despite continued conservatism in their operations. She described this as related more to 'the desire to achieve a convincing image of perennial newness, of global attention and of postmodernity' achieved through new plans and renovations for existing museum sites (2006a: 39). Message's work cites Fredric Jameson's critique of the colonization of the cultural sphere by corporate capitalism, and the 'the frantic economic urgency of producing fresh waves of ever more novel-seeming goods' (Jameson 1991: 4). Architecture is noted as the closest of all the arts to the economic, presaging the turn to architectural newness in museums like the ROM. Message framed the museums' discourse of newness as 'publicity', which is the making public or 'opening to public view' of information, often, as noted by Ku (2000), to garner public opinion and credibility. Message also suggested that 'new' museums have incorporated the other 'new museology' positions that advocate social reform and multicultural dialogue in their *rhetoric* of newness, but not in their form and practices (2006b: 12). Thus the publicness evoked by such publicity takes on a new sensibility: publicness as celebrated and cutting edge, 'being new, exciting, and relevant today' (2006a: 29).

In public

Attracting public notice using the language of newness in their profiles, plans, and publicity is a crucial observation about museums that contributes to a final form of publicness relevant to this study. Message's interpretation of new museology as modern museums getting 'publicity' describes, at a very basic level, the process of bringing an event or person to the attention of 'the public' in an 'in public' performance. The public–private/open–hidden qualities of communication described above also invoke this kind of performance as an act of publicness.

Two aspects of this sense of publicness are of interest here. On one level, performance can be viewed as an 'in public' act that serves to mask or hide that which is kept private within (Shryock 2004). Museums are out 'in public' all the time, making public representations or performances through their exhibitions and other communicative forms. These can be seen as a public face put on in society, celebratory, and aesthetic. National museums frequently project rhetorical images in their displays without discussing complex issues or more sordid controversies (Sharma 2015). The growing role of media-centric conceptualizations of publicness, with its dependence of publicity and representation, and de-emphasis of face-to-face interactions among publics, contributes to this masking tendency (Ku 2000; Splichal 2006). The result is a sense of being 'in public' where agents in the public sphere perform their selves on a symbolic level, masking more complex interiors, with each interacting through a public face.

On another level, the attracting of public notice has become a performance of status or celebrity. Hannay (2005) maintained that the public sphere has been turned into a playground, to which people escape from private lives to gain some pleasure from others' 'in public' performances. He criticized the media as no longer a site of sustained democratic attention or collective expression, a position he attributed to the conversion of citizens (or publics) into homogeneous consumers. This is a critique that has been at play since Adorno criticized the culture industries, Debord theorized society of the spectacle and the commodification of experience, and Jameson elaborated aesthetic production as commodity production in late capitalism (Adorno and Horkheimer 2000; Debord 1971; Jameson 1991). A highly mediated celebrity culture, in place of the deliberative public sphere, offers visibility and credibility to certain public agents. The vast opportunities for voyeurism and illusions of intimacy, give those watching a sense of the 'real' and the 'special', thus conferring legitimacy to those who appear to be high status (Van Krieken 2012). Those being watched employ image, rhetoric, icons/brands, to project public aura and

Debordian spectacle. Such 'in public' performance has long been a staple of museum existence. But some museums appear to have combined their corporate communicating and pedagogical exhibitioning to tap into this publicness-as-celebrity. The impact on publicness-as-democratic-interaction has been the elevation of the celebrity sphere as a place where real political issues – from cancer research benefits to climate change campaigns – have been played out and shaped agendas and debates. One questions then that, if visibility – seeing and being seen – trumps negotiation and relationship-building as the means used to build public knowledge and decisions about matters of concern, does it truly serve the public interest?

3 'Renaissance' and the ROM in public

From 2000–2008 the Royal Ontario Museum had entered a crucial stage in its history, undertaking a redevelopment project worth more than $300 million, billed as a 'Renaissance'. As the lead project in a 'cultural renaissance' in Toronto, aimed at positioning the city as an international cultural capital, it was one of a number of high-profile museum expansion projects across the globe in that decade (Message 2006b). Under the guidance of star architect Daniel Libeskind and dynamic new director William Thorsell, the ensuing RenROM project restored the museum's heritage buildings and galleries and created a spectacular landmark, the Michael Lee-Chin Crystal, sparking a city-wide, even nation-wide, storm because of its design.

This project offers a powerful case study of the reinvention of a traditional museum amidst contemporary social changes. The renaissance was to be achieved through a two-stepped process: transforming the physical shell and its public spaces within, and, significantly altering what Thorsell called 'the public side of the museum' by creating an 'agora'. For Thorsell, the agora would actively facilitate peoples' engagement by 'getting out there and not being afraid' of controversy. But as circumstances and conditions evolved throughout the project, controversies erupted, and a politics of mission and positioning dictated the nature of the renaissance.

This chapter offers some insights into the history of the museum, and the ideas and processes behind the RenROM project. The ROM is the most well-known museum in Canada because of its long history, the breadth of its collections, numbers of visitors, and international reputation. Since its establishment in 1912, the purpose of the museum, its physical structure, its management and its publics have slowly changed, reflecting, to a large extent, broader historical trends experienced by 'universal' museums in Western countries, and changes in the social, economic, and political conditions in Toronto and Canada.

Originally operated within the University of Toronto as five separate museums devoted to archaeology, geology, mineralogy, palaeontology, and zoology, the Royal Ontario Museum was rooted in Victorian-age interest in progress, science, industry, and God; the social value of knowledge and education; and the desire for civic respectability and status (Teather 2005). The key founders, archaeologist/collector Charles Trick Currelly and financier/university patron Sir Edmund Walker, did not want a regional institution, but a Canadian research museum of international stature (Mak 1996). Currelly's international-calibre connections and stunning archaeological finds stocked the museum's shelves (Currelly 1976). This was a time when huge numbers of objects were lifted from far-away places and deposited at the new museum without attracting moral and political uproar. The Currelly antiquities were combined with collections of other University of Toronto curator-professors to form the core of the new museum. But the excitement and interest engendered by the more spectacular aspects of the collections, combined with its civic-enhancement goals, gave the museum an additional, more popular framing. From the beginning, there was an alliance, and a constant tension, between the academic and the civic/popular, in terms of the museum's governance and people's perceptions of its purpose in society (Duffy 2006). The public aspect of the museum's early existence meant catering to the popular enthusiasm for unique things people had never seen before and seeking to enlighten and civilize a provincial population.

The Renaissance

In 1999, the ROM had crafted a strategic, long-range master plan to expand and update its crowded facilities and revitalize the museum's public image 'to help sustain the Museum into the next millennium' (ROM 2000: 23). William Thorsell was appointed in the summer of 2000 as Director and CEO to lead the project. He was a career newspaper editor at Toronto's *The Globe and Mail* but was hired as a man with a vision who could build support (HR specialist, 5 July 2010). Thorsell presented the Renaissance ROM project in September 2000 as 'a process not of renovation, but of transformation' (ROM 2001: 23).

The redevelopment process through to 2006 involved an estimated cost of $200 million, with $150 million to come from private or corporate fundraising (figures that changed through the process of construction). A high priority was placed on retrieving the heritage buildings of 1914 and 1933 'in all their architectural glory' as well as creating a new public gallery space to be designed by a prominent architect. After a highly publicized international competition with more than 50 entries, a short list of 12 and three finalists, the provocative design by the Berlin-based studio of virtuoso architect Daniel Libeskind was chosen. Libeskind was renowned for his work on the Jewish Museum in Berlin, Germany, the Imperial War Museum North in Manchester, UK, and the World Trade Center site in New York. He proposed adding 170,000 square feet of exhibition space within a 'Crystal' design that combined 'five interlocking, self-supporting prismatic structures' linked to the original ROM building with bridges. The exterior was to be primarily clad in glass (later revised to primarily silver brushed-aluminium because of construction problems). The architecture also introduced Libeskind's 'deconstructivist' interior aesthetic, characterized by acutely angled walls, dead ends, constrained corridors and asymmetries (Libeskind 2001). The new Crystal was a huge construction project in its engineering complexity.

In December 2005, ten renovated galleries in the heritage buildings were opened, including the Chinese gallery and the First Nations gallery. The new addition, the Michael Lee-Chin Crystal, formally opened (without exhibits) in June 2007 with a Big Bang Party that attracted 1,000 invited guests and a horde of 22,000 spectators over that weekend (ROM 2008). From December 2007 to the spring of 2008 galleries were incrementally unveiled. The project had increased the total public space to 388,000 square feet, including new public galleries, new facilities for education and public programmes, and new amenities such as a restaurant, gift shop, and a large lobby (ROM 2006).

William's vision

ROM directors had a long history of absolute power within the institution, and the director's vision has always been inextricably linked to the museum's goals and performance. The charismatic Thorsell was no exception, and the sheer power of his vision for the museum was cited constantly during this research by all members of the organization. The ROM was a hierarchical organization where decision-making power rested with the senior management team, including the director who held considerable power at the top. This style of museum leadership is what Janes (2009) calls the 'lone director' model. According to Janes, the 'lone museum director model is an increasing liability in these complex times' because the lone director can be cut off from honest reaction and feedback which could lead to isolation, overburden, and impaired or myopic judgements (2009: 62). Under Thorsell, the director model was not coercive, but it was hierarchical – as a departmental assistant suggested 'the buck stops with William' (Executive assistant, 2 December 2009).

The RenROM project thrust the museum into the public eye in an unprecedented way with a spectacularity of architecture and verbosity of language that propelled the institution into celebrity status. But the director also boasted that his RenROM project would be a different museology: not only a new building and a new vision, but a new way of doing a museum. Thorsell's new vision had two parts, both of which set up the ROM as a prominent and active mediator of the public realm. The museum was to first get as much of the collections as possible on display, to show off their richness and beauty in a striking piece of architecture that would achieve the status of world-class for the museum. The 'in-public' nature of this building itself, as a showpiece, was central to Thorsell's vision: 'The Royal Ontario Museum offers a singular opportunity to create a new star in Toronto, Ontario and Canada ... to retrieve the old and invent the new at the centre of Canada's leading metropolis', he said (Thorsell 2000). He was adamant that the way for the museum to survive was to create what he called a 'landscape of Desire', thus gain support because of its enhanced consumerist and celebrity status (Ross, 13 April 2006).

The energies of the organization, including Boards, management, and staff, were keenly focused on this architectural project until 2007, when Thorsell articulated the second part of his vision, moving from what he called the 'hardware' symbolic form to 'software' (Thorsell, 5 November 2009). In May 2007, the director announced in his speech to the Empire Club in Toronto that the museum would be repositioned as an 'agora', a cultural common where assembly, debate, and discussion could take place. He pointed out that the idea of agora was a trend in museum culture world-wide, driven in part by institutional survival – the need to generate revenue in light of declines in government support – but he also felt this reflected social responsibility. Museums were now the saviours of cities, he declared, because of this functioning as common ground and agents of provocative conversation. Thorsell described it this way:

> On the public side of the museum – what we interpret it now – our obligation is to not just be passive on the issues of cultural change and the environment. We have skill sets there, we have mandates there. So we need to get out there and not be afraid of hosting good strong discussions about these things and confronting or uncovering or even providing a spot to talk about these things.
>
> (Ibid.)

So, late in 2008, the ROM changed its branding logo to 'Engage the World' as the overarching philosophy of the new, revitalized ROM (ROM 2009). By late 2009, the director reflected on the importance of 'communities', emphasizing that through the intensive fundraising efforts to support the new building, he discovered that 'meeting new communities, meeting new people, bringing them in, we realized that is *not* just fundraising, *that* is the nature of the museum' (Thorsell, 5 November 2009). Engage the World thus meant a literal engagement with all the cultures of the world.

The redevelopment propelled the ROM into an unprecedented public prominence in the minds of ordinary Torontonians. For William Thorsell, the debate and passion provoked by the Crystal was evidence of its success as a piece of public culture (Bradshaw 2010). The news media at the time generally praised the Royal Ontario Museum as a beautiful tool to achieve the much-desired status of world-class city for Toronto. The museum was a place for visibility – an agent that symbolized status, legitimation, and signification of greatness on the world stage. As evidenced in the news media, the RenROM's new, in-your-face architecture did raise the public profile and image of the museum, and stimulated discourse around its nature as local and international celebrity (in April 2008, Condé Nast Traveler magazine listed it as one of the seven architectural wonders of the modern world).

The architecture acted like a public art installation which, as Thorsell claimed, elicited spirited public debate. The announcement of the success-ful bid by Libeskind was followed by letters to Toronto newspapers con-demning the design because of its exploding-glass aesthetic, a huge departure in sensibility from the staid brick and stone original. In the local Toronto press, architectural critic Lisa Rochon wrote:

> It's hard, aggressive and in your face. It cantilevers dangerously over the street, shifting the ground from under our feet. Do not expect shelter from the $135-million Michael Lee-Chin crystalline addition to Toron-to's Royal Ontario Museum by Daniel Libeskind. Expect the exaltation of one architect, one man, one individual. Expect the stuff of Libeskind: an exile, a brilliant thinker, a marketer with a silver tongue …
>
> (Rochon 2007)

The use of architectural expansions in order to re-stimulate stagnant museums has been widely criticized in museum literature. According to Morris,

> A new or expanded museum building is frequently seen as the fast track to reinventing the museum. Working with a star architect is con-sidered a guarantee of success in assuring a prime leadership position among cultural attractions in the community, or even in the country.
>
> (2007: 102)

Morris said that while the 'BHAG (Big Hairy Audacious Goal)' was considered a prime measure of success in some organizations, it also included many risks, such as unrealistic expectations, poor definition of scope, underprepared board and staff, and poor synchronization of physical and programme plans, which could leave a museum unprepared for operational difficulties (2007: 104).

Here was a new building and a new vision, but in what way this instigated a 'renaissance' in the museum's practices is the subject of enquiry of this book. The description of purpose employed by Thorsell appeared to use an explicit interpretation of the word public: a sense of publicness that actively facilitated peoples' engagement with matters of concern. The radical scene of public assembly I witnessed 'in public' outside the ROM was an extreme demonstration of the kinds of societal issues that were pressing on the public side of the museum. Thorsell's reputation in the press was that of an instigator of radical change who would not put up with 'intellectual compromise' (Bradshaw 2010). Would Thorsell's positioning move the museum beyond collecting and displaying and educating, to 'get out there and not be afraid' of controversy? This change of emphasis warranted critical inspection because it implied an important role in democratic practice. The following chapters explicitly investigate how this revisioning through the RenROM project rearticulated its ways of being public, interfacing publicly and serving diverse publics. This brings the 'museum in focus' during this intense period of development in order to demonstrate the complexity required for museums to act as sites and agents of social change.

Part II

The ROM in public

4   Positioning

How a museum positions its relationships with external publics is the first indicator of how it understands its public role. Who it engages with, what public face is presented, and how relationships are managed are all important elements. In this chapter, the ROM's *positioning* with stakeholders, publics, and other externals are scrutinized as 'public relations': communicative activities defined as 'the strategic management of relationships between an organisation and its diverse publics, through the use of communication, to achieve mutual understanding, realize organizational goals, and serve the public interest' (Flynn *et al*. 2008). The invocation of relationship management, publics and the public interest in this definition clearly identifies this process as a useful way of looking at the public nature of the museum. The positioning the ROM adopted, and the public face it presented in relation to outside publics and other organizational entities, involved several departments under the mantle of Marketing and Major Exhibitions, but influenced strongly by the ROM Board of Governors' office. This chapter looks for evidence of a renaissance in the way the ROM defined its publics for corporate relationships, and in the public character of the museum's interactions in this area.

The use of the term 'public relations' (PR), is important to describe the nature of the publics addressed in these communicative activities and the type of relations they embodied. Both imply a who and a how that are very specific. The nature of the ROM's public relations was noticeably business-like and elite in character and was dominated by a category of publicness that invokes the performance of status or celebrity: being 'in public'. Being in public in this sense was a branding activity that stressed the marketing of positive or celebratory messages, but also harkened back to the historic role of museum-going and museum patronage as a sign of social status. The chapter explores how the ROM's corporate interactions were controlling, ranking, selling, or engaging, depending on how and at whom the museum positioned its activities, and how these related to its publicly stated positioning as agora. It focuses on the targeting of ethnic communities as stakeholders during the renaissance project.

Public relations, in the context of systems theory, enables an organization to establish mutually dependent relationships (Cutlip *et al.* 2000: 228). But there is an ongoing tension between theories of public relations that stress its 'management' function, that is, the control of information, and its 'democratic' function as a social and dialogic process (Thurlow 2009). Thurlow sees PR as a 'management function which evaluates public attitudes, identifies the policies and procedures of an individual or organization with the public interest, and plans and executes a programme of action to earn public understanding and acceptance' (2009: 249). However, Wehmeier (2009) points out that in real-world usage, 'communication management' has emerged as the dominant concern of practitioners. Thurlow calls this management of information, 'spin doctoring', which is the control of information and public opinion (2009: 250). She admits that while public relations might be perceived as the way corporate, political, and ideological groups distort issues, confuse voters, and manipulate public opinion to serve their own interests, instead, public relations is *ideally* about building relationships and promoting informed opinion and action.

Pearson (1990) looks at this tension as an ongoing philosophical interplay of *strategic* values in opposition to *ethical* values within an organization. The tension is reflected in the way individuals or groups are defined and treated: the first involves the containing and management of people into definable roles and relations as 'stakeholders', and in the second view, 'publics' are unorganized (and uncontrolled) people brought into relationships with the organization (Mackey 2006). These discussions within public relations also reflect the foundational work of Habermas (1984) who saw 'strategic action' to orient opinion within the public sphere (the work of PR) as attacks on the ability of publics to associate and communicate in an unregulated manner.

'Publicity' is a common public relations process employed to achieve a positive positioning for an organization. In the case of museums, attracting attention in positive ways helps them accomplish certain goals, demonstrating that they are reaching public service objectives, providing value for money, increasing attendance, promoting products and programmes, or making publics feel good in various ways. Attracting attention through publicity can accord benefit but also can be detrimental, especially if 'bad' publicity harms an institution's public image or even threatens its mission. Publicity is also linked to the concept of 'celebrity', a state of publicness that implies widely circulated public recognition or reputation, or as Coombe describes it 'a floating signifier invested with libidinal energies, social longings, and political aspirations' engendered by the media and public relations (1991–1992: 365).

Ambiguity between public relations and marketing is common because they share communicative practices such as publicity, and because marketing increasingly emphasizes the point of view of the customer (or the public) in relationships. How public relations and marketing each defines their publics is a crucial point of differentiation. Mackey (2006) is concerned about the way that the word stakeholder had invaded public relations language in a way that implies a shapeable audience or sellable client. Many writers have critiqued the invasion of consumerist, management, and neo-liberal language and practices into public service and non-profit organizations (Newman and Clarke 2009). Other scholars emphasize that defining and relating to stakeholders enhances both the legitimacy and accountability of publicly funded institutions, and help to define the 'public value' (Scott 2009) and 'cultural value' (Holden 2006) of institutions like museums. But Mackey argues the denotation of stakeholders instead of publics implies those who 'have been figuratively drawn, or at least are imagined to be, inside the tent as co-conspirators of the power centre in the middle of the organizational system diagram' (Mackey 2006: 8). Within the tent a stakeholder can be co-opted and silenced, or as insiders, have the power to influence agendas. 'Active publics' are sometimes perceived as threats to the strategic interests of the organization that require 'issues management' through PR (Ledingham and Bruning 2000: 18–19).

Within museums studies literature the positioning of public relations and marketing in museum settings tends to be prescriptive more than analytical. An explosion of interest in marketing emerged in the cultural sector in the 1990s (Gilmore and Rentschler 2002). Since then, there has been a great deal of instrumental concern with studying what makes successful marketing, and the role of PR within those processes (e.g. Minkiewicz *et al.* 2014). Janes' *Museums in a Troubled World* (2009) is among the few publications questioning the normalization of such marketplace-based public relations/marketing/managerial ethos.

The ROM and its stakeholders

During the RenROM project, the museum positioned itself corporately in relation to various external stakeholders with whom it wanted to engage. But all stakeholders were not perceived as equal. How each was weighed by the museum potentially influenced decision-making, resource allocation, and ultimately how the institution presented itself as public. The institutional need for continuous private donations, for example, appeared to influence who was prioritized as a stakeholder and how relations were conducted. ROM stakeholders tended to be those who are well educated and well connected more so than those who were disadvantaged or disconnected. 'The public', that is, general visitors and people outside the museum, might technically have a 'stake' in its operation as a public institution within a government Act and partly funded by government. But those ROM departments devoted to communications (including marketing, corporate communications, public relations) treated the public differently in their activities than other more definable groups.

Groups who received public relations attention at the ROM included museum members, donors, 'community' groups, other museums, and governments. 'Members' were an early form of stakeholder at the museum – enthusiasts who have always been given various insider benefits in return for financial support. The museum's positioning towards members migrated from a service relationship to a sales and marketing orientation during the RenROM years (Senior manager, 27 November 2009). Responsibility for front-line services for membership, volunteers, and visitors worked closely with the Governors and the annual giving and patron programmes. Responsibility for membership was shifted to a Marketing, Sales, and Membership department, which was later called Marketing and Major Exhibitions:

> What's happened now is that Membership officially became part of Marketing. And the premise was that every ticket revenue generator, whether it be membership, whether it be full price, whether it be promotions, whether it be groups, that average, that per cap, that you're looking at for revenue generated by your visitors, however you define those visitors, is now managed under one umbrella.
>
> (Senior manager, 27 November 2009)

This move positioned Members as marketing *objects*. 'Memberships' became a crucial sales product, important to the financial survival of the museum, rather than a category of relational *subjects*. General museum membership, historically a mark of exclusivity, experienced a corresponding reduction of status and benefits. Only those who purchased costlier, higher-level memberships retained their high status and access to special 'insider' benefits.

The pressing need for financial support often drove decisions about which publics' interests come first, and the nature of the museum's positioning towards those stakeholders. The Renaissance ROM Campaign fundraising effort by the ROM's Governors set precedents for their public relations work in relation to donors, with high-quality communicative materials and events produced both to solicit sponsors and benefactors, and to reward them for their contributions. The communications between the museum and corporate or elite patrons might be described as glowing, with press releases and promotional material endorsing sponsors in grateful terms (e.g. ROM Governors 2009). Those who donated or sponsored were rewarded with public demonstrations of their select status with the naming of buildings and galleries; inclusion in Royal Patrons and Young Patrons Circles (YPCs) with accompanying benefits; prominent positions in all communications; 'first-in-line' status at public events and programmes; and insider inclusion in social galas, curatorial behind-the-scenes contact, and celebrity events. The Governors' PR and communicative relations underscored their elite nature, tinged with the language of marketing and advertising, but evoking a sense of privilege and 'world-class' status in their public positioning of favoured stakeholders.

One sub-group of members who were also regarded as essential but different stakeholders, were 'communities' or ethnic groups. The encouragement of ethno-cultural groups demonstrated mixed desires on the part of the museum for broader-based sponsorships and audience expansion, as well as relationship-building with non-typical publics. The ROM had a history of relationships with ethno-cultural communities through Friends groups, a formalized means of denoting and managing social inclusion, but also a way in which groups themselves are able to collectively manage their self-representation. The groups, as with any public, had mixed needs of their own, from genuine desire for new educational experiences, to the aspiration for Canadian cultural capital and elite status, to the need for a public stage for presentations (Volunteer 7, 27 May 2009). Such Friends groups gave special benefits to their members, publishing newsletters, creating programmes, and contributing to ROM exhibition and programming activities. As with the broader visiting public, the Friends were themselves only representative of certain segments of society that correlate with the elites present in the rest of the ROM membership categories (ibid.). The ROM and the Friends devised a range of public relations and marketing activities aimed at drawing 'communities' into the museum. Informal observations indicated, for example, a very strong South Asian presence during special programme days and Friday Night half-price admissions.

While communities were desired as active subjects, they also become objects for fundraising and marketing. A museum administration handbook in those years unabashedly characterized ethnic groups as 'one of the hottest new markets' and advised 'museums that are not already doing should begin marketing to these groups not only in order to better serve and increase audiences, but to cultivate future financial support'

(Grenoways and Ireland 2003: 256–257). During RenROM, the Governors' office targeted such ethnic cultural groups for fundraising, to the point that 'community consultations' once perceived as cultural sensitivity projects were managed as fundraising opportunities – the Dead Sea Scrolls exhibition advisory group was a case in point, presented as consultative, but who personally contributed $150,000 towards the scrolls exhibition in 2010 (DSS Minutes, 24 March 2009). 'Heritage communities' as marketing targets could be seen as an exhibit for publicity: for example Korean Heritage Day, developed for self-representation and social inclusion, was featured in marketing literature as an exotic exhibit for others. Communities themselves were caught up in a somewhat conflicted positioning by endorsing and promoting such marketing efforts. It was unclear whether the relationships that minority members formed with the Friends indicated a community-building and confidence-building exercise, or an ethical inclusion of their cultural practices by the museum onto its public stage, or a commercial manipulation and up-selling that took advantage of ethnic ties.

Processes of relating

Interactions between institutions and stakeholders can take many forms – sponsorships, consultations, collaborations, partnerships, participation, engagement – all of which imply different types of subjective positioning and communicative relations (Davies 2008). The processes deployed in these relationships can be characterized as controlling, ranking, selling, and engaging – important indicators of how the museum interpreted its relational positioning. *Controlling* denotes habits of authority and gate-keeping exercised through the director that controlled the communicative relationships with external publics. *Ranking* suggests the ROM's use of fundraising and publicity to emphasize status and celebrity. *Selling*, and its associated actions of marketing, advertising, and customer service, emerged as a primary internal focus and concern during the RenROM project. The final indicator, *engaging*, implies the new vision expressed by Thorsell, which would necessitate a dialogic subject positioning on the part of the museum. The corporate positioning of the ROM in public relationships sought to control, offer status, and try to sell or encourage dialogue and engagement.

Museums have historically started from a position of power where they were in control of the message, trying to shape not just public opinion, but public behaviours. The first inclination of any corporate communications group is to control messaging, including the communications that go out of an institution, and to some extent, the information that circulates within the institution. In recent years, control of corporate communications in museums has become more formalized under the business/managerial model of management with the perceived need to plan and measure a museum's performance (Zorloni 2010). Releasing control and the sharing of information dissemination has been a central debate in museums generally, usually with reference to how exhibitions are developed (e.g. Lynch and Alberti 2010; Morse *et al.* 2013). The sharing of the control of corporate museum communications has only marginally been discussed.

The control of information was key to the positioning of corporate communication and relations with the public during the RenROM development. The methods employed to do this reflected standard corporate practices: news releases, launches, events, media relations, and external monitoring (Communications coordinator, 5 July 2010). But issues of control came to the fore in the embarrassing University Tower incident, where, in 2005, the ROM was forced by a vociferous local community to back down on a condo development on museum property. While corporate PR released glowing accounts of the proposed development, the museum was unaware of the state of the relations with its external publics. Local media captured William Thorsell's public embarrassment in hostile town hall meetings. The University Tower misstep surprised him and altered the museum's subsequent dealings with these people who had not been identified as stakeholders. In this case, the museum learned something about one-way versus dialogic public relations processes: what began as a confident display of plans to an audience perceived as compliant, evolved into a consultation requiring dialogue because of confrontations.

While control was the most obvious positioning of the ROM's corporate face, their fundraising and publicity activities also reinforced ranking, that is, a positioning that emphasized status and celebrity. Tony Bennett (2006: 54) has written extensively on the way culture as a 'social sorting mechanism' has been mobilized by museums, and by people themselves within museums. He questions whether the inherent ranking mechanism has been changed by museum rhetoric and the 'scholarly illusion' of cross-cultural and cross-social exchange and engagement. At the ROM, corporate messaging consistently emphasized a promotional tone of best, biggest, 'newness' and world class, carving an image of the museum as celebrity. Even the Engage the World tagline, from its earliest appearance in corporate communications, seemed to be more about world status than world connection, consistent with the celebrity the museum wanted to generate around the Crystal as a public icon. This inevitably targeted those publics who sought social affirmation or legitimation, or to somehow bask in the glow of the museum's renown. Fundraising was an activity that implicated the museum's inherent ability to bestow cultural capital though selling a 'stake' or through a non-financial association. More crassly, being associated with celebrity gives one a feeling of being a 'player'. The museum was hailed as the best event venue in the country, because of its star quality.

The solicitation of financial stakeholders through the selling of status is accepted museum practice and was a basic strategy of the Renaissance ROM fundraising campaign. What was new for the ROM was including ethnic communities to provide some of the money, as noted above. According to Thorsell,

> Half of those names on the wall downstairs of major donors who have pictures are first generation immigrants. Half of our supporters at more than $5 million each are first generation immigrants.
>
> (Thorsell, 5 November 2009)

Thorsell's position was that combining fundraising and social inclusion was a natural fit. For their part, ethnic elites were buying North American-style respectability, status, and cultural capital.

Donors and patrons who supported the museum are uniquely rewarded by gaining access to the museum as a very public stage. Such visuality is vitally important to publicity and the idea of celebrity – being 'seen in public', as well as its downside – being exposed to the 'harsh light' of publicity (Iveson 2007). In corporate communicating, either positioning has the effect of attracting attention, thus can contribute to museum public relations and marketing strategies. The normalizing of celebrity as an accepted part of the ROM's cultural language, and an acceptable positioning for its corporate communications, was also reflected in the museum's programme and events. The primary Institute of Contemporary Culture exhibits and programmes in 2009 were *Vanity Fair Portraits* and *The Question of Celebrity*. The promotion of the Terracotta Warriors' Directors' Signature lecture series included the tagline Leadership, Celebrity and Spirituality! described as 'a series of lectures by great thinkers that explores the timeless allure of power, celebrity and spirituality in our world, both past and present'. The Young Patrons' Circle's annual PROM fundraiser for 2010 offered 'a thrilling night of dark glamour and cinematic fantasy' in an old Hollywood setting, proclaiming that 'these young, wealthy patrons will be treated as celebrities' (ROM 2010). (Tickets for this fundraiser were $275 for YPC members.)

Priorities and decision-making in the museum at the time were affected by this selling and buying of status and celebrity. Decisions about time, space, and the allocation of resources increasingly tended towards the provision of revenue-generating exhibitions and special events. Selling was intimately connected to the museum's positioning of 'controlling' and 'ranking' in their external relations, eventually subsuming and making expedient both message-control and status-enhancement as part of its mechanism. Staff did not, in their interviews, have any problems with controlling or ranking stakeholders and publics. But they instead were very concerned with the way relations were being transformed by marketing initiatives, including the reconfiguring of museum collections into marketable content, the transformation of visitors into consumers, the translation of engagement into sales transactions, and the converting of community consultation into audience development. Marketing and the promotion of attendance and revenue, normally the province of for-profit organizations, dominated the ROM's external corporate communications, more so than the creation of goodwill and moral interactions, the classic position of non-profit PR as defined by Turney (1998).

The true public impact of the Renaissance ROM project was the creation of a new museum brand, selling a new sense of place as celebrity. Rethinking the brand as an essential marketing strategy was crucial for the ROM, to get away from its 'fusty old museum' image from the past. On a strategic scale, the ROM took an integrated marketing approach that aligned all aspects of the museum's functions to generate paid attendance or revenue (Visitor Relations specialist, 20 May 2010). The museum's communications in this perspective were less about public relationships with certain stakeholders, than serving a more integrated marketing offer. The museum reorganized its departmental structure and altered its Board policies to emphasize exhibitions as an integral part of marketing.

The strategic approach of smooth and integrated alignment made sense in the ROM's corporate and executive offices, but chafed on the collections and education side. Staff voiced concerns about the invasion of a marketing perspective, some reflecting on a concern that museum collections would then be perceived as 'products' to buy and sell, rather than having intrinsic value. Tlili (2008) noted the way institutional language often divided museums into 'corporate' versus 'mission' sides of the organization, one associated with attendance and government priorities, and the other with core audiences and traditional museum functions. A long-time ROM employee characterized this trend as the museum 'moving from a museological focus on content to a marketer's focus on visitor wants and needs' and added, 'the pressures are such that, if the topic is popular and will bring people in, then that topic is given more resources than a smaller topic with less ability to bring people in. It's very marketized' (Exhibit planner, 11 December 2009). The re-labelling of the programming department in 2009 as 'Programme and Content Communication' appeared to reinforce this worry.

A marketing orientation emphasized the wants and needs of users. 'Customer' is the focus here, not 'public'. Marketing positions stakeholders and the general public as consuming clients, and customer services become the focus of most museum energies. Visitors, of course, were highly analysed at the ROM, subject to three kinds of visitor research: exit surveys, visitor satisfaction cards, G7 studies (Marketing coordinator, 4 June 2010). When visitors or audiences see themselves as customers or consumers the museum's visitors are then more inclined to look for 'their money's worth' (McCracken 2003). Their public experience becomes less about looking and seeing or being there, and more about 'consuming' more and newer things (Janes 2009). In my ROM encounters with visitors as they came through the entrance gate, those who paid daily rates were very concerned about maximizing their expensive visit. As one ROM manager observed, when a public is seen and sees itself as 'just a market' instead of a public with whom the museum has 'some kind of higher mission to engage with', then those attitudes will prevail in all levels of the relationship (Exhibit planner, 11 December 2009). The translation of 'engagement' into market relations shifts corporate positioning to an emphasis on attendance development. During the RenROM development, the museum's galleries, lobby, and lecture halls were increasingly marketed for events like wedding receptions or business events. Hosting these brought in significant new revenues – 185 per cent greater in 2009 than the year before (Thibault email, 26 October 2009).

What happens to the 'public' in this equation of positioning/stakeholders/relations, and where does publicness come into play when stakeholders are perceived as a commercial group of some kind? The ROM's attitude appears to foreground 'private' or at least 'commercial/ corporate/consumerist/capitalist' in its orientation. The sense of publicness created by this new type of visitor orientation was perceived by some staff and visitors as intrusive and jarring, taking precedence over other public functions. Staff were forced to adjust to conflicts over uses of museum public spaces, such as wedding receptions in the central Currelly Gallery. The implication in the minds of staff and volunteers was that there had been a shift in corporate culture: that business and special event customers were the new priority audiences, general publics were less important, and corporate positioning was reoriented towards those stakeholders.

A new public positioning?

A final characteristic of how a museum positions itself in relation to its publics and stakeholders, is 'engaging', a positioning introduced in the new vision expressed by director Thorsell. When asked to define the brand of the museum, a ROM visitor relations employee said,

> The ROM brand right now is really about the question of, we want to engage you. We want you to feel that the ROM is for everyone. 'Engaging the world', that whole concept.
>
> (Visitor Relations specialist, 20 May 2010)

But the message of engagement was not strongly evident in the museums' various public relations, nor in the discourse in local newspapers. The museum's positioning during RenROM emphasized information control, enhancing status and selling celebrity, and soliciting attendance: Thorsell's new vision of public programming and the agora has been lost in the glare of publicity. By the summer of 2010, corporate communications avoided the word 'engage' altogether, although it was the registered trademark. The word 'access' was used frequently but in terms of disability and 'exclusive access', implying patron's and member's insider privileges.

Engaging as a way of building public relations is dialogic in nature, a very different stance that requires, as Kent and Taylor elaborated:

> *mutuality*, or the recognition of organization–public relationships; *propinquity*, or the temporality and spontaneity of interactions with publics; *empathy*, or the supportiveness and confirmation of public goals and interests; *risk*, or the willingness to interact with individuals and publics on their own terms; and finally, *commitment*, or the extent to which an organization gives itself over to dialogue, interpretation, and understanding in its interactions with publics.
>
> (2002: 24–25)

These are the assumptions that underlie the concept of engagement as a dialogic public relations positioning. Mackey (2006) argues that if public relations *is* more about dialogue and the positioning of an organization in the democratic milieu, then the notion of 'uncontrollable publics' is more fitting than the notion of 'stakeholders'. These aspects of positioning and communicating are encompassed and analysed within Chapters 6 and 7 on Exhibitioning and Interacting. There, the discussion details how the ROM positions itself in relation to 'publics' who are not defined as groups or corporate entities or stakeholders, but as 'the public' in a sense of diverse individuals or visitors served through publicly oriented interfaces of 'engagement'.

5   Structuring

How publicly a museum operates is embedded in its organization of spaces, resources, processes, and practices. Such publicness is rarely a front-of-mind decision by most museums. Institutional organization of knowledge and public space underpins and shapes its public nature. This chapter describes in more detail the connection between these *structuring* aspects of the ROM and the articulation of a new public role being offered by the director. Anthony Gidden's idea of 'structuration' is referenced here, and how social, cultural, and organizational norms, and physical limitations of space, situate and contextualize human and institutional practices (Mosco 1996). Structuring of any sort might be considered an antonym to the ideal of publicness, in the sense that spontaneous or chaotic interactions or practices are institutionalized and instrumentalized. But how and why such structures exist and work, and how they frame and codify certain ways of looking at the world and types of interactions, gives interesting clues as to the importance of, and constraints on, the public nature of any institutional communications. The chapter introduces such factors as the constraints of the physical plan and infrastructure, the organizational model, its operational processes, and economic issues, all of which might not be considered to affect publicness in the usual way. As explored by Gray and McCall, understanding underlying structures in museums – of bureaucratic power and authority, relationships, work rules and processes, relevant actors, and informal cultures – allows an explanation of how choices are made (2018: 126).

Several theoretical perspectives link structure and the public nature of museums. The innate power of institutions like the museum to structure human subjectivity is a recurring theme in the literature, whether theorized as ideological apparatus (Althusser 1971), hegemonic authority (Gramsci 2005), or monopoly of knowledge (Innis 1951). The museum is one of those institutions, such as the family, the media, religious organizations, and the education system, holding 'symbolic power': they act as important places for the accumulation of information, communication, material and financial resources, and shaping the ways in which information and symbolic content are produced and circulated in society (Thompson 1995). Museologists have come to realize that they 'generate ideological effects for constructing and communicating a particular vision of society' (Sandell 2007: 3).

Some researchers have applied Michel Foucault's theories on the structuring effects of institutions to museums as technologies of social control, that is, ensembles of discourses, mechanisms, and apparatus that act to create particular social meanings and subject positioning (Foucault 1991; Hooper-Greenhill 2003). Tony Bennett's foundational sociological text, *The Birth of the Museum* (1995) suggests that the social governing mechanism of being seen in public spaces like museums acted to 'civilize' the actions of social players – a place where people appeared in the social gaze of others and performed 'how to behave in public'. This played an important role in structuring hierarchies of difference within museums. Bourdieu (1984) reinforces this perspective, describing for example the essential role of art museums in establishing the social and cultural capital that maintained bourgeois class status in 1960s France. The use of museums for social status differentiation and legitimizing has been an ongoing topic in museum theorizing, drawing attention to the way that people's actions are influenced, not through direct intervention, but through cultural and psychological effects inherent in institutional spaces and processes.

Status structuring

Bennett's insights into nineteenth century functions of museums strongly apply to the ROM when it was founded in 1912: Toronto's very wealthy families supported the international collecting expeditions of Charles Currelly, the first director, and supported the establishment of a museum because they desired the civilizing of Toronto residents and the enhancement of the city's international profile (Mak 1996). But even today, visitors, staff and society at large still unquestioningly consider the ROM to be not only a place for 'world-class' information (the preserving and display of collections), but also a significant location for improvement and social status enhancement (the appearance and improvement of people). One critic remarked 'William Thorsell's genius – the genius that precipitated his appointment in June 2000 – was to flatter moneyed Toronto's aspirations' (Nuttall-Smith 2008: 57).

The underlying question of 'who' as a structuring element in the public nature of the ROM critically links 'who appears' to questions of 'who

governs' and 'who benefits'. The question of 'who' was reflected and perpetuated through the museum's embedded systems (little changed since
1912) of patronage, governance and programming. Kelly's 2008 study of
RenROM noted the promotion of the museum as a 'natural' centre for elite
culture as well as the increased use of public branding techniques to draw
attention to donors. The museum's Board of Trustees and its primary
patrons continued to be wealthy members of society. In the first seven
years after 2002, the Renaissance ROM project had raised $166.5 million
of private donations, including a Lead Gift of $30 million from business-
man Michael Lee-Chin (ROM Annual Report, 2009). The most generous
patrons had buildings and wings named after them and played active roles
in governing the museum. This was not new for the ROM (or any other
major museum) – as Kelly points out, this appears to be a continuing of
traditional ways of being. However, such structures of governance and
patronage affected the public nature of the museum, and whose interests
were served. The Board, while they acted on behalf of the public, were
themselves members of a small portion of that public. Although efforts
were made during RenROM to solicit multi-ethnic Board members and
patrons, each was drawn from the same privileged social bracket.

While Toronto's social elite were primary donors and governors of the
museum, the character of its visitors also continued to reflect dominant
social groups in the city and the province. This is a social and cultural norm
that highly influences the public functioning of many Western museums.
Studies of visitors during RenROM portrayed the average visitor as well
educated, middle-aged and female with a higher income – earning more than
$75,000 a year (Marketing coordinator, 4 June 2010). The traditional
museum visitor who fits this general profile also brought with them strong
perspectives about how a museum 'should' operate. This was the public who
the museum served: the core museum visitor came from a small segment of
society; understood, and was highly influenced, by the structuring codes at
play and was likely to reproduce those ways of understanding and of acting.

Recognizing the inequality of this form of audience, many efforts were
made to broaden the profile of users. William Thorsell realized that the
new users would come from what he called 'communities':

> The fundraising required us to go out and communicate, cultivate new
> communities ... Now they are on our boards, they are on our fund-
> raising groups; they are on our Friends groups.
>
> (Thorsell, 5 November 2009)

It is interesting to note the tone he took here: 'communities' was code for
Others. This sense of separation was reflected within the language of the

museum's annual reports, for example '... we will feature the art, music, spirituality and cuisine of different cultures in the city – much of it produced *by them* [italics mine]' (Royal Ontario Museum 2007: 6). Such a comment not only reinforced a we–them stance but characterized 'cultures' in a stereotypical way (Mullard 1985). And while new communities were slowly becoming involved with the museum, one staff member noted that the new ethnic patrons and volunteers still fit into the structuring relations of class:

> We always have served the people who are better educated than most and have higher incomes than most. We've always done that, since the beginning of time ... That doesn't change with ethnic diversity.
>
> (Exhibit planner, 11 December 2009)

The question of money

It is an obligation of critical theory, wrote sociologist Craig Calhoun, to ask reflexively about what underpins the institutional organization of knowledge in the public sphere. Calhoun argued that *the* critical questions to ask about whether an institution is 'public', is how knowledge is produced and circulated, and whether money is an omnipresent organizational focus (2006: 10).

Any organization is constrained by financial issues of revenue and allocations, which can frame how it operates. Janes argued that the financial vulnerability of most museums has resulted in a harmful fixation on money and a 'preoccupation with the marketplace and commerce, characterized by the primacy of economic interests in institutional decision-making' (2009: 94). Fundraising dominated the ROM's activities while the Crystal was being planned and constructed – the Renaissance ROM Task Force's budget in 2002 was $200 million. As of 2009, the Renaissance ROM Campaign Cabinet led by Hilary Weston had raised $280 million in private and government funds, oft-repeated in the ROM's literature as 'the most successful cultural fundraising campaign in Canadian history' (ROM Governors 2009; Thorsell, 16 December 2009).

A focus on money continued to affect the museum's decision-making, according to many staff members. Two factors appeared to contribute to this: although capital funds were available, limited operational funding constrained programmes and practices, and, there was a shift towards a business/corporate ideology by the board and senior management which affected the ROM's priorities and operations. The second factor created an ideological shift in understanding the 'public value' as set out in the museum's mission statement. Weinberg and Lewis argue that public value should not be 'decided strictly by market forces as they are in the private sector, but through politics and public deliberation about what is valuable' (2009: 261). But during the research, the language of value used throughout the museum emphasized management, control, and business metaphors. Managerial forms of governance privilege business and governmental logics in decision-making, treat stakeholders as economic agents, and exert pressure towards quantitative indicators of performance (Newman and Clarke 2009: 128). Public value is then assessed through measurable indicators such as attendance, number of exhibitions, earned revenues, cost per visitor, and so on (Janes 2009; Zorloni 2010). The ROM's Board of Trustees, with its corporate and elite profile, was likely to assess public value and make decisions from a managerial perspective, and be inclined to regard its economic stakeholders (patrons, funders) as primary 'clients' to whom they were accountable – notwithstanding their legislated accountability to 'the public'.

Attendance and the search for numbers was the most important objective at the ROM during the RenROM period. Public value, by inference, meant the sheer number of people who came through the door. As Knelman (2009) opined, 'Attention-getting expansions by celebrated architects (Daniel Libeskind at the ROM, Frank Gehry at the AGO) were supposed to be magic solutions to the numbers issue'. This kind of external discourse contributed to how people would think about and discuss the museum, thereby shaping public opinion. It was reflected internally at the ROM as well, where the ideology of money and attendance appeared to drive decision-making. As one middle manager bluntly stated about the culture within the organization, 'It is not public trust driven, I would say. It's more, at the moment, attendance driven … So abstract discussions about the public trust are sort of irrelevant … the everyday takes over' (Exhibit planner, 11 December 2009).

Thus, the entrance fee became a key structuring element at the museum, shaping the quantity and quality of access to the museum. General admission tickets in 2010 were $24 per person, plus $16 for children aged 4 to 14. Concern about admission fees came up frequently in interviews with staff, management, visitors, outsiders, and with the director (Thorsell, 11 November 2009). Physical access to the building, as a common property of the public, should be a fundamental characteristic of the publicness of the ROM – access to the collection, access to the space, access to the intellectual content. But while the museum made efforts to mitigate its high entrance fees through subsidies and memberships, overall, this underlying financial structural barrier limited public access to the museum, and thus the quality of its publicness.

Structuring organizational hierarchies

Institutions also perpetuate ideological, symbolic, disciplinary, and regulatory structuring power within their organizational discourses, systems, and practices on the ground. Such 'material practices governed by a material ritual' are practised by and on subjects (in the case of a museum, those who work and visit the institution) who consent to and perpetuate such practices (Althusser 1971: 160). Bourdieu (1990) described such practices and rituals as 'habitus' – dispositions or acquired aspects of culture that are reflected in individual daily habits, and that generate and regulate social life. The culture of an organization reinforces a habitus in its operations, where behavioural and relational norms are maintained through a complex of infrastructure, rules, procedures, and communications. Capra (2004) wrote that while such structures are needed for the smooth and efficient functioning of complex organizational systems, this makes flexibility and openness and change more difficult.

Gray and McCall (2018) emphasized the way that bureaucracies continue to be the dominant system for organizing and managing work within museum institutions around the world today. Robert Janes argued that most large museums are unable to change creatively or demonstrate 'resilience' – subtlety, agility, and adaptability – because they suffer from bureaucratic inertia and are subject to marketplace ideologies (2009: 141). But public institutions require such resilience, constituted with transparency of process and openness to external demands, in order to be 'public'.

In the case of the ROM, resilience was also needed internally, as the Renaissance ROM redevelopment project changed the way the museum operated and put serious strains on ROM workers. Said one employee, 'For some people it has been a trial by fire … This has been the greatest example of change management that could ever be conceived' (Visitor relations specialist, 20 May 2010). The managerial form of governance at the ROM, which used quantitative performance indicators and business-modelling results-based planning, was adopted to rationalize and bureaucratize administrative systems at the museum (Communications specialist, 12 July 2010). Formal structures of the museum's organization – particularly managerial ideologies and systems, and the professionalization of museum work – changed hierarchies, relationships, and ways of doing things. However, the effect of this kind of results-based practice was the tendency to orient the organization towards project-based or individual job-related goals, rather than public or externally oriented goals. This influenced the public interfaces of the museum: its attitudes towards the public, the publicness of its practices, and the nature of its public offerings.

Policies, procedures, and departments, as well as the physical environment, were reorganized to reflect the new director's vision. Management teams of a few senior staff, such as the Integrated Planning and Programming group and the Marketing Team, were clearly the key decision makers. Janes identified unequal and controlling hierarchies as a major source of workplace dysfunction and himself employed a flat, egalitarian approach that encouraged self-organization (2009: 71–77). Gray and McCall found that hierarchical bureaucracy was a source of frustration for staff in most museums. They cited an attitude among staff at lower levels that 'whatever happened at senior levels had either no real relevance for undertaking the job or that there was little that could be done about it anyway' (2018: 129). Interviews with some workers and curators at the ROM indicated frustration with their lack of input into senior management decisions (e.g. Staff interviews, 19 August 2009, 27 April 2010, 5 May 2010), and a staff survey in winter 2010 specified that 40 per cent of employees did not have 'overall satisfaction' with the workplace and cited 'communications' as a problem (Koester email, 18 May 2010). Parker (2014) notes that when staff encounter problems with institutional change, or when its speed causes stress, unhappiness is inevitable. Proposed solutions like 'enhancing communication' are often wrongly interpreted as just communicating louder and more frequently. At the ROM, the hierarchical reporting system coupled with top-down decision-making was often the issue, resulting in the privileging of some voices and neglecting of others, coupled with the new managerial and sales orientation. As one curator stated, 'in terms of determining what goes out there [on the floor], it is very management driven; and *now* it's management and marketing-driven' (Curator A, 3 May 2010).

The museum's organizational culture was structured within its bureaucratic systems, but was also affected by its human power relationships. Gender and race as well as hierarchical status position underlay institutional attitudes, which, in turn, shaped the agenda and knowledge-building processes at the museum, and affected the public face put forward by the ROM. Power dynamics existed among all who came to the table to build public knowledge, both inside and outside the museum. But sharing authority and building consensus requires addressing the ways that organizations are multiple, contingent, and divided (High 2009).

Workers themselves had vested interests in protecting power hierarchies. Grenoways and Ireland (2003) flagged the challenges faced by museum administrations, including multiculturalism and sexism, but one of their suggested solutions – professionalism – might instead lead museums *away* from developing a renewed attitude about their role and practices as public institutions. Professionalism plays a part in the structuring of an institution, but it also might serve to erect boundaries between staff members, and reinforce hierarchies of difference depending on expertise. Professions are exclusively organized occupational groups whose members share a common occupational identity and commitment, and also have control over what their work is and how it is done (Tran and King 2007: 135). It is usually considered a positive thing in the museum field, and its promotion has been a long-standing function of museum associations. But professionalization can structure rigid functions and cultures within an organization – for it can be a self-governing and largely closed community of practitioners who have the power to determine the standards for organizational relationships and practices (Cheney and Ashcraft 2007; Menand 2009). Professionalizing can affect the public nature of the museum because it leads to the exclusion of other knowledge builders: the public takes a back seat to the efficiencies of professional regulation. Professional criteria reflect and shape particular kinds of social relations and expectations that might, for example, exclude other cultures or resist building new or creative ways of knowledge-making.

At the ROM, the professionalizing-effect was quite prominent in the divisions between curators and educators, but also within the public education function itself, with divisions between educators, programme facilitators, and volunteer docents and interpreters. 'Education' was something one did with children, as opposed to 'programmes' which was what one did with adults, or, what one did with kids in camp or in a club programme format. Volunteer programmes and activities were a third category of people offering public programming, but they, too, were separate in their training and techniques. All three groups looked down on the quality of public programmes offered by each. Curators, too, had a professional shape, and they were upset if that was changed, for example, by being drawn into public programming.

Structuring public space

But structuring the publicness of a museum does not only occur through human actions. Institutional organization of spaces can underpin and shape its public nature. In the case of the ROM, the redevelopment project was, first and foremost, an architectural one, creating a new space that would attract public attention and focus the public dialogue about what the ROM's place should be in society at large. The spectacular new Crystal affected people's attitudes and ways of being in the museum both inside and outside the museum. Described as a collision of old and new, it was perceived as an architectural dialogue or as a conflict: a 'landscape of desire' or 'assault on the street', depending on the viewer. The controversial architecture was a dominating influence in how employees, visitors, neighbours, and anyone else perceived the nature of the museum's renaissance.

In simple terms, the spectacular architecture attracted visitors who just wanted to see it – 22,000 people attended the June 2007 opening of the new building in its first weekend (ROM 2008). Though reactions were mixed, all eyes in the city were turned to this iconic public building that profoundly altered Toronto's cultural landscape. The intent of ROM management was to enter the public sphere with a 'bold vision' that set a particular tone for the public nature of the museum that was more than simply a container to house collections and conduct scientific research. 'Beyond its significance as a cultural institution, the Museum is now branded because of its connection with a star architect', wrote Kelvin Browne (who was also the Vice President of Marketing and Major Exhibitions during the project) in his book *Bold Visions*. By promoting architecture as an attraction for tourists, 'a building, even if its contents may not interest them, is a *must see*' (Browne 2008: 51). Thorsell himself emphasized the liberating potential of the architecture as exhibitionary statement. He said,

> You walk into this museum and it doesn't feel like 'oh this is a museum for Europeans'. It doesn't feel like that … It is not neo-colonial, British, European. Because that's our thing, it had to be a global statement; it had to be an inclusive statement. That's the way I've always thought about when we were choosing the architect. That this statement about the museum had to be dramatic and everything else, but it also had to be inclusive in the sense that it's nobody's heritage – we are creating heritage. We are not copying anyone.
>
> (Thorsell, 5 November 2009)

Experts offered a more critical view on the architecture and the physical spaces it created. One professional in the museum field shrewdly pointed out it was a 'landmark building' not a 'landmark museum', panning the functionality of the architecture (Expert, 15 April 2010). Celebrity or vanity architecture has been the subject of museum academic critiques (Hudson 2006; Morris 2007). Kylie Message detailed the global 'new museum' trend, exemplified by the Bilbao Guggenheim, as not simply about constructing spectacular buildings, but as a symbolic and rhetorical assertion of 'being postmodern'. She suggested that while, physically, such museums project relevant and exciting images of 'newness', they exist, instead, as deeply compromised and complicated by historical factors and bureaucracies (2009: 605).

Observations about the new Crystal's *interior* spaces were expressed from two points of view: a continuation of pleasure in the aesthetics of the architecture, and concerns about its utility. Toronto Star urban design writer Christopher Hume (2007) called it a 'marvelously respectful relationship between old and new' that 'halt[ed] the dumbing-down of the institution'. The new structure added an estimated 170,000 square feet of exhibition space in new galleries, and a huge flexible space, described as 'one of the largest exhibition halls in North America', designed for the temporary blockbuster exhibitions (Browne 2008: 40). The gallery space within the new building was 'all about walls that lean precariously and join together sharply' (Hume 2007). This angularity deeply affected the sense of space within the museum and was frequently the subject of debate by staff and visitors who voiced more practical concerns. The most obvious constraint was on exhibition style: without upright walls, objects had to be in free-standing cases, or, like the dinosaurs, free-floated on plinths (Curator C, 15 June 2010). Kelvin Browne celebrated 'the sense of joyful disorientation' people experienced in the entry hall and retail area (2008: 40). But the unusual spaces and connections in and between the new and old buildings, especially the reliance on stairs and ramps, made circulation and way finding extremely complicated for users and subject to numerous visitor complaints. A worker complained in frustration,

> To me that should have been in the planning stage: 'how do visitors get around the building?' Why weren't ramps put in? Why were there stairs everywhere in this day when people have troubles walking, when you have these huge SUV strollers? It was like there was no thought of people other than single or childless, able-bodied people … Like when the Crystal first opened, people couldn't work out how to open doors! … So, there is a huge disconnect in the architect's design.
> (Programming worker, 19 August 2009)

Other physical constraints created by the new building were infrastructural – a lack of temporary galleries; not enough seating throughout the buildings; the absence of washrooms in the new structure; conflicts over the use of the limited programming space among departments; a lack of places for children's activities, especially in the basement exhibition hall; hard-to-reach lighting in the new building; and even raccoon problems high in the upper floors of the Crystal. Staff corroborated that corners were cut during the RenROM project because of time and budget constraints, all of which affected the quality of the galleries, the public spaces and the ability of public programmers and educators to do their job (Education supervisor, 27 April 2010).

The most-mentioned example of how the new architecture structured experiences, as expressed by visitors and by front-line staff, was the entrance lobby. The lobby was the premier public interface in the museum. Yet its design was unwelcoming and confusing. The narrowness of the entrance doors and circulation at the front entrance was a concern during architectural design (Vaughan *et al.* 2009). Confusion at the entrance was discussed by most visitors interviewed, including one who could not identify the location of the front entrance from the outside, another who could not figure out how to open the doors (a problem also mentioned by security guards). Visitors entered a low, aesthetically unappealing area with a ticket sales desk. The floor sloped upward from the doors through a soaring lobby at the junction of the old and new buildings. This amorphously shaped lobby had multiple archways of various sizes leading to the lower level exhibition hall, the 'Stair of Wonders', the retail shops, the 'Spirit House', the main elevator bank, the separate entrance to the formal restaurant, and the stairwell that led to the lower cafeteria and upper floors. Visitors tended to be baffled about how to get out of the lobby with its multiple apertures.

However, overall, visitors interviewed in the study were positive about the architectural transformation, although they were a bit more reserved about the configuration of space in the interior. On one extreme, a first-time visitor from Montreal commented that the new architecture was 'white, naked, bare and cold' while another from Newfoundland exclaimed 'Awesome! The way it's done, oh my god!' (Visitor interviews, 1 May 2010; 15 December 2009). Others were more equivocal, 'It took some getting used to ... I think it is good. It gets out of the mindset that it's a dusty old one-hundred-and-some old building. I like the Crystal more and more each time we come in' (Visitor interview, 14 December 2009). Said one retired woman, 'Some of these ultra-modern architectural things – I just wonder if there is an element in it of the Emperor's New Clothes, you know?' (Visitor interview, 22 December 2009).

Clearly the architecture presented something novel and disruptive: a new public face playing a different, unmuseum-like tone in the public realm, which can be interpreted as disorienting or confusing but can also be read as exciting, innovative and inclusive. 'The public', that is, people outside the ROM looking in, were truly affected by the iconic architecture of the Crystal and many admitted, in informal conversation, to visiting because the building was a '*must see*'. Their public experience of the architectural space instilled an impression that stayed with them as they encountered the exhibitions inside – the subject of the next chapter.

6 Exhibitioning

Exhibitioning is a mode of publicness for which the museum was clearly mandated. Exhibition settings within museums are public spheres, where people gather to socialize, be educated and entertained, and talk about ideas. Displaying is a public act that is both communicative and aesthetic in its methods of making meaning, offering multisensory and embodied opportunities for engagement (Schorch 2013a). But exhibitioning is not a neutral act; it can be perceived as a public positioning as the last chapter suggested. As Sharon Macdonald pointed out in her essay on museum theory, an exhibition is a suggested way of seeing the world and a statement of position (Macdonald 1996; Whitehead 2016).

This chapter follows the previous discussion of the structuring of public spaces at the ROM, which were conceived as part of the 'hardware' of the museum, and focuses on the public nature of its exhibitions, perceived by museum management as part of the 'software'. The ROM began redesigning all of its galleries in 2002, and launched in 2009 an ambitious five-year plan for special exhibitions. The new galleries, temporary displays and blockbuster exhibitions are discussed here as public communicative texts, and whether and how stated intentions were translated into physical form through the RenROM design process. The nature of the exhibition spaces, how the displays communicated, and what public experience and engagement they offered, are inspected.

The public positioning of the museum through exhibitioning is illustrated through an analysis of the blockbuster exhibition on the Dead Sea Scrolls that inaugurated the ROM's new museum space and announced its intention to Engage the World. This exhibition blurred the line between exhibiting as something the museum always did to communicate with the public, and marketing as something the museum did for sales and business development. The public reputation of this exhibition also carried a political weight within the international community that invoked a combination of prestige, intellectual respect, strategic advancement and financial profitability. The chapter concludes with an analysis of how ROM management chose to 'engage' with an external political challenge from nontypical publics demanding transparency in addressing the controversial topic of Palestinian history.

Exhibitioning must be understood within current debates about the role of exhibits as communication and cultural forms. Research into museum display as a media of communication looks at both the encoding and decoding that occurs: how exhibits are produced, how they communicate as texts, and how viewers learn, perceive, and construct meaning (Dicks 2000). As Stuart Hall points out, an exhibition provides a 'framework for interpretation' using three-dimensional objects on display to create meanings which, knowingly or unknowingly, reflect the perspectives of its creators (1997: 3). Museum exhibitions can also be understood as a type of public ritual that, by their very authority as institutional, can solicit, draw in and focus people's attention (Couldry 2003). Tony Bennett has written extensively on the way that museum exhibition, from Enlightenment times, imposed order and hierarchy on ideas, and emphasized rhetorical modes of communication (see Bennett 1995, 1998, 2006). Objects were the central items of importance – whether artefact, specimen, or art – protected and studied by an authoritative curator. It was not until the 1970s that cultural history museums turned towards mimetic display techniques with objects in reproduced environments and narrative texts with thematic storylines. Such displays relied extensively on the reading of text expressed in a passive, anonymous, institutional voice (Coxall 1997). Sometimes 'discovery rooms' with assortments of curios displayed in settings that encourage touch were also employed. At the Royal Ontario Museum, the showing of collections of objects employed the more scientific stance up until the 1970s, when a more interpretive communicative style was integrated into an ambitious gallery planning project that redesigned most of the museum's spaces (Lockett 1991). The ROM moved from rows of armour and insects on pins, to narrative display approaches such as room settings, thematic cases and panels, complex dioramas and demonstrations of museum research processes.

Eilean Hooper-Greenhill (2000a) has elaborated on the way museum exhibition functions as a visual communicative medium, devoted to the social and cultural practices of showing, looking, and seeing. Exhibitioning can be seen as a visual discourse enabling communicative relationships between presenter and viewer. While those doing the presenting embed a complexity of meaning, a complexity of meaning is also read into the viewing, depending on the looker. But I have argued that what is being presented drives the discourse more than the meaning-making desires of the viewer – in all types of museum display the end goal is to manage and direct the attention of the viewer (Ashley 2010). In its position of authority, the museum sets the agenda for the audiences to follow and tends to focus its efforts on ensuring the audience comes away with a preferred meaning. Thus the 'in-public' nature of exhibitioning as communication involves 'putting on view' more than 'let's talk'.

To look at the museum exhibition is to look at both sides of a communicative exchange: the designer and the viewer, each making meaning in their own situated way, communicate through this medium, the exhibit. Henning observes that 'Exhibit designers give great consideration to visitors' engagement by organizing and controlling viewpoints and pathways through the exhibits, and by careful arrangement of space within the exhibit' (2006: 55). But what viewers or users *do* with public exhibits offered by museums must also be considered, even within the shaping effects of institutional exhibitory techniques, tropes, and embedded contexts. The 'general public' is a diverse group of people who go to museums for social outings, education, leisure, boredom, debate, discussion, and countless other reasons. Many studies point out how people bring their own viewpoints, social circumstances, and educational backgrounds with them to construct a museum-visiting experience. My informal observations at the ROM indicated that people attended according to their own wants and needs, often despite the promotions aimed at them. They chose a variety of viewing techniques from hunt-and-peck to detailed reading of labels. They were solitary as well as present in extended families, and brought silence and reverent whispers as well as a noisy cacophony.

In general terms, visitors' exhibition experiences are myriad, and not always according to the goals of the institution. Grant McCracken (2003) points out that many visitors resist any external structuring of their visiting habits and prefer to be left to their own devices, albeit this inevitably occurs within the selecting, framing, and organizing of materials that any display of objects offers. The exhibitionary experience, for most people, is an embodied one within public spaces (despite virtual museums) and entails visual and non-visual sensory interactions. On any day at the ROM, from my observations, the public clearly demonstrated their preference for the hands-on galleries: without fail they asked the front-entrance volunteers how to get there. Those galleries were always busy, and people's attentiveness to exhibit content was consistently evident.

Exhibitioning and RenROM

The new permanent galleries of the ROM were conceived to fit in with the challenging architectural tone and unconventional public exhibition spaces posed by Libeskind's design. From the onset, the proper display of artefacts and specimens was presented as a key motivation for the redevelopment, and the ROM's rhetoric about the aesthetic style of the museum had an effect on the public nature of the new museum. There has been extensive research on the effects of different methods of museum display. Kirshenblatt-Gimblett (1998) discusses two principles of display that come into play at the ROM: the first describes more traditional use of glass cases and wall displays to demonstrate and teach, and the second uses simulations or reconstructions to give a more immersive sensation of a broader context that draws in the viewers. The first emphasizes 'the gaze' of the viewer, which Henning described as 'an abstracted act of looking, characteristically disembodied, distanced and assured', while the second encourages 'gaping' or 'gawking' as spectators become involved in 'a sense of wonder or embodied experience' (2006: 54). Lord wrote that these two exhibitioning approaches are sometimes divided into the either–or oppositional logics of 'aesthetic' versus 'anthropological', where the first is object-based and the second is narrative-driven (2007: 356). The aesthetic approach is both decontextualized and ahistorical, counter to the story-driven, narrative approach taken by the anthropological method (2007: 355). Duncan (1995) felt that in the aesthetic model museum space is more elitist, while in the anthropological perspective, which she calls the 'educational' model, the museum space is seen as more democratic and popular.

Museum theorist Kylie Message (2006b) argues that late modernism encouraged the more elitist 'white box' idea of the museums as a 'sanctified place for the contemplation and enjoyment of high art externalized from culture', especially from culture understood more anthropologically and produced by mass media (2006b: 81). Such differentiation separated art museums as cathedrals 'offering a pure aesthetic realm produced from universal ideas of taste and removed from both cognitive and ethical spheres' (ibid.). Here, as theorized by Bourdieu, aesthetic appreciation was normalized as the inherent 'culture' of the bourgeoisie (Bourdieu and Darbel 1991). The trope of the 'aesthetic', according to Message, removed such exhibitionary spaces from more narrative, historicizing forms of popular culture but, worth noting here, might also have removed the museum experience from the ethical/moral realm. Such aesthetic detachment might then allow the exhibit to side-step dealing with controversial topics and political engagement (Marcus 2000).

Despite the more populist and interactive trend within contemporary museums, the new RenROM galleries strongly took an aesthetic approach that foregrounded the objects in the ROM's vast collection. 'Museums should be creators of art as well as guardians of artefacts and specimens' wrote Thorsell in 2008. Chris Nuttall-Smith highlighted the director's oft-repeated objective of creating 'a landscape of Desire' (2008: 57), and wrote that 'William looks at objects as masterpieces. He does not believe in a dynamic interaction between the visitor and the display. So displays are art museum displays; they're at a distance from the viewer' (2008: 60). This principle was transcribed throughout the design of the new galleries.

Newspaper critics were mostly critical in their reviews of the new galleries (e.g. Nuttall-Smith 2008; Rochon 2007), with some reviewers supportive of the galleries' spectacular spaces (Hume 2007). Nuttall-Smith quoted Gail Lord, an international museum consultant, who observed,

> The Royal Ontario Museum is the only major museum in the world that has taken the view that the vast majority of exhibits should consist of artefacts in cases ... There is no other institution that I know of that has so consistently returned to the Victorian notion of the museum.
>
> (Nuttall-Smith 2010)

Some ROM staff voiced criticism to the aesthetic orientation of the galleries. An education employee summed up her impression as 'they are not educational galleries, they are art galleries', and elaborated on the galleries' limitations as teaching resources:

> I have issues with trying to teach eco-system connection in a gallery that aestheticizes.... There is something about aestheticizing nature because it is quite beautiful. On the other hand, there is a way in which they have completely militated against diorama to such a degree that some of the displays are really quite incomprehensible. For instance there is one display that is supposed to show an old rotting log, and the different animals that depend on that log for shelter. They can't actually use a rotting log – too diorama-like – they are actually using a grey box. Try and explain to a child ... It looks like a sewer pipe!
>
> (Education worker, 10 June 2009)

An exhibit planner acknowledged that the galleries reflected a 'design-oriented aesthetic vision':

> Well I think they're very beautiful. I think they're very traditional, and I think they lack narrative and ... they're too crowded, I think, and it's difficult to discern where one finishes and the next one begins. So I don't think they're particularly successful ... I think they're sort of museology of 20, 25 years ago.
>
> (Exhibit planner, 11 December 2009)

The viewing habits of visitors support this critique: in a 40-minute period observing visitors to the Gallery of China on 4 June 2010, of 74 people entering the gallery, only four spent any time looking intently at the gallery displays. Most people were silent as they walked through or used low voices, except for one crying baby in a stroller; I noted several yawning. Visitors employed a hunt-and-peck method of browsing, stopping ten seconds to view a piece then strolling on. Several paused to take photographs or pose for them. Not one looked at the introductory panel texts near the entrance. Ten people were on a guided tour and attentively listened at each stop, although few closely scrutinized the tour-leader's choice of artefact. While my observation cannot account for the motivations of individuals, the visitors on the whole appeared just to 'be there' in this public space, rather than engaging in more focused attention or intellectual inquiry. The beautifully arranged objects seemed simply the wallpaper of the redesigned space, a backdrop for a pleasant stroll and photo poses. The public experience in this space was passive, with no clear activity of engagement or participation with the displays or with other visitors.

Designing the galleries

The actual production process employed by the ROM to build their new galleries reflects what happens to the rhetoric of 'renaissance' and 'world-class' and even 'engaging the public' in the face of the real task of designing and building a huge number of exhibitions. How this affected the public character of the museum is explored here, through a description of the gallery development process. The management of gallery development influenced the public nature of the galleries – the quality of the public spaces, the transparency of decisions made, the publics who got to participate, and the ways in which the exhibitioning in the galleries served the public interest.

William Thorsell began his tenure in August of 2000, and by October had shifted master planning emphasis to iconic architecture and design principles that invoked open spaces and object-focus, without a 'clutter' of information (Curator X notes, 11 February 2002). At that point, the main galleries were to hold eight to ten 'jewel rooms' of 'beautiful objects' which would focus on space and seating with one or two sets of objects in an atmosphere like a 'pristine chapel' (ibid.).

Gallery design was seriously underway by June 2002 when the Board of Trustees established the Renaissance ROM Task Force and approved British design firm Haley Sharpe Associates as exhibit designers. The initial budget for gallery design was $72 million: they hoped to raise $60 million from governments, $14 million in private funds, and $10 million from the sale of the ROM's planetarium site. Installation was targeted for spring 2005. In an important all-staff memo in April 2003, the director laid out his vision of the public nature of the galleries, formulating his 'engage' objective but expressed in terms of access:

> It is our public responsibility to bring out of the storage rooms the best representatives of our main collection in a manner that engages and informs the visitor. The ROM is not a 'theme' museum, which relies on something other than collections to engage the public. We are engaged by our collections.
>
> (Thorsell, 8 April 2003)

He went on in this memo to lay out his philosophy for the design of public galleries in the language of 'access': access to collections; sensual access; intellectual access; and psychological/emotional access. Target visitors would be 'adults who are curious about the world, and their families' (ibid.), and 'curious families with superior knowledge and students with some prior knowledge' (Curator X notes, 3 April 2003).

The museum adopted an extremely tight planning and design schedule, including rough concepts of all galleries by December 2002, schematic designs one year later, and detailed designs for most galleries about six months later (Barnett 2003). The opening of Phase 1 galleries (those in the older building) was scheduled for December 2005, and Phase 2 for December 2006 (ibid.). One of the challenges of getting the project done so quickly was that the building design and the gallery design had to be done simultaneously. This pressure to get things done quickly and to make many adjustments during the design phase had to be addressed throughout the project and compromised some of the results. For example, architectural limitations were unrecognized in two-dimensional plans, and there was a lack of time to properly model the spaces in three-dimensions. One curator fought hard during the summer of 2004 for a three-dimensional model of her gallery and finally persuaded the in-house design department to do so. The model proved a useful tool for detecting unexpected issues, such as slanted architectural pillars that obscured public viewing.

The tight schedule may have also affected the number of employees who were allowed to be involved in the project. There was little internal consultation about the design of galleries, and only some curators were enlisted as part of the planning team. 'It was speed, it was efficiency', according to a senior manager, so some staff 'were kind of boxed out of it' (Senior manager, 4 March 2009). The challenge of the tight planning schedule might also be the reason that 'objects not narratives' was adopted as the design approach, and why the public's point of view was not clearly incorporated within the planning process. The consequence was a form of exhibitioning adopted in these galleries, whose public function was simple and decorative, more than complex and communicative.

Objects not narrative

The catchphrase 'objects not narrative' was repeated in various forms throughout the planning phase. Haley Sharpe's focus throughout the process was on the collection of object lists – core objects, 'star' or iconic objects, oddities and curiosities, and new acquisitions (Ruitenbeek 2002). The design company produced a communication strategy in December 2003 to direct 'an integrated exhibit planning and creative design framework for the whole Renaissance ROM project', where they reiterated:

> as a general principle, it is the World-class collections of the ROM that are driving the exhibit design process, rather than arbitrary themes or stories … Each object selected for display is meant to be seen, looked at and thought about … Nevertheless, each gallery should have a distinctive character and style; whether a group of artefacts is an eclectic mix exploring context and connections or is assembled to tell a story, the methodology described in the communication strategy will be applied.
>
> (Haley Sharpe Communication Strategy 2003: 1)

This appeared to generate an ongoing tug of war between the designers and the curators. One of the interviewed curators complained, 'It was an inadequate process and inadequate timing … It was one of the most frustrating things I have ever done', and compared the process to 'disaster planning' (Curator A, 3 May 2010). Working with the offshore contract designers often meant their curatorial work was just one piece of an efficient machine churning out galleries.

Throughout 2003 and 2004 there were disagreements over lack of storylines, choice of objects and images, layouts and texts, and particularly the lack of consultation (Curator X notes). The curators were told by Haley Sharpe, 'we design at distance and that is why we were hired – for the way we work' (Curator A, 3 May 2010). The notes and emails saved by Curator X reveal that this tension came to a head in June of 2004 when the curators received their design development packages from Haley Sharpe. A group memo from all curators was sent to senior management in protest over the design packages, which said 'The consensus is that the quality of the design packages and the case layouts they contain is poor'. They noted

'The quality and prestige of the new ROM is at stake'. The memo even cited their curatorial employee agreement as their authority to request more design input. They concluded their memo by saying 'it would be very sad if, inside the new architecture and heritage buildings restored to their original beauty, the public would find galleries that are mediocre or less'. The letter stimulated the immediate response of more consultations with designers, and a request from the Vice President of Collections and Research for summaries on the 'state of the galleries' so that 'the meetings with Haley Sharpe can be as constructive and productive as possible'.

Two areas of 'public' interest that were neglected during the rapid design phase were community consultation, and front-end and formative evaluations of the galleries. There was uneven involvement of external publics throughout the design phase. The museum hosted public forums at various points in the project to present gallery design concepts. Curatorial-led consultations tended to focus on gaining the advice of experts. The African galleries, for example, were subject to extensive consultation, but participants were academics, rather than people from the African Canadian community (Curator B, 3 May 2010). Despite these attempts at consultation, there is no visible evidence in the museum, other than in the First Peoples' Gallery, that external publics cooperated in the creation of gallery content or design.

The second area of neglect lay in the formative evaluation of the galleries. The ROM was once a leader in doing front-end and formative testing of designs, texts, and media during exhibition development (Lockett 1991). While audience research to assess general visitor satisfaction was undertaken by Marketing (Marketing coordinator, 4 June 2010), there was no evaluation after, before, or during design that considered how to improve the galleries from the public's point of view.

Galleries were opened to the public with an 'architectural opening' or limited preview of the Crystal architecture in June 2007. A sequence of Crystal gallery openings began with the dinosaur exhibits in November 2007. Gallery completion took longer than planned, mostly due to architectural delays, and curators described numerous 'deficiencies' in the galleries as unveiled – objects or images or texts or labels or other media that were not installed for many reasons (Curators A and B, 3 May 2010; Curator C, 15 June 2010). Journalist Val Ross remarked on these deficiencies:

> When the ROM's elegant new Asian and first-nations [sic] galleries opened earlier this year, the display labels were so confusing; more than 1,000 of them had to be redone by the designers, Haley Sharpe of Leicester. Thorsell had thrown his weight behind a ROM committee

awarding this company, one of the world's most prestigious, a $10-million contract for exhibition design ... [Visitors] complained that the labels were confusingly placed, hard to read and didn't offer enough information to satisfy their curiosity.

(Ross 2006)

This account of the galleries' aims, design, and development process, and the impressions of insiders and those external to the ROM, suggests a particular understanding of the 'crystalline' quality of the museum's new gallery spaces and content. It is tempting to read Crystal-as-metaphor – outwardly the Crystal was a public statement of radiance, transparency, and luxury which appeared to symbolically transform the museum. But inside, the exhibitionary content appeared cold and precious, housed in temple-like public spaces, filled with detached simplicity, not story-telling complexity, and designed in opaqueness, not clarity.

Exhibitioning hierarchy

There is a striking contrast in public sensibility between the aesthetically styled permanent galleries and the more nuanced temporary displays that almost all used more interpretive and narrative approaches in their exhibitioning. On an annual basis, temporary or changeable exhibitions at the ROM included one large A or blockbuster exhibition per year in the Garfield Weston Hall in the lower level of the Crystal, one main exhibit in The Institute for Contemporary Culture on the fourth floor of the Crystal, several types of mid-sized exhibits throughout the museum, and small object rotations within individual galleries. Exhibitions were considered curator-based, community-based, iconic-based, or profit-based, depending on their public purpose.

An example of a mid-sized exhibition was *Stitching Community: African Canadian Quilts from Southern Ontario*, which occupied the Canadiana short-term exhibit space from January to September 2010. The exhibition used historic quilts to discuss the role of African Canadian women in Buxton, Ontario, a community established by freed slaves who settled in Canada, and included quilts, photos, dolls, and other small objects plus a video of quilters recounting stories. This temporary exhibition was intriguing because it was curated in collaboration with an external group, it adopted a narrative and story-telling exhibitionary style, and it imbued the aestheticized Canadiana gallery with some warmth. *Stitching Community* was an example of a ROM's Community and Regional exhibits, aimed at giving voice to community groups, and to 'develop new audiences and support group sales' (ROM, n.d.). The community consultation involved with this display was aimed at social inclusion and cultural sensitivity – the desire to build bridges with Black community groups can be seen as part of the legacy of the controversial *Into the Heart of Africa* exhibit (Exhibit planner, 20 November 2009). Shelley Ruth Butler, in her review of *Stitching Communities*, said the small exhibit 'speaks to the permanent gallery' and 'compliments a curatorial strategy of de-centering the two founding nations myth of Canada'. She further commented:

> the Canadiana Gallery is overwhelmingly silent on the social history of African Canadians, including such issues as slavery, the Underground Railway, abolition, segregation, racism and Canada as a meeting ground for different cultures, long before official multiculturalism. *Stitching Community* is a useful corrective to this situation, though it does reinforce a standard narrative that celebrates Canada as a land of freedom, without addressing in detail, the nuances and contradictions of this claim. Nevertheless, *Stitching Community* represents an important step in recognizing an early black presence in Canada.
>
> (Butler 2010)

The human perspective that this display brought to the Canadiana gallery cannot be overstated. The 'feel' of this exhibit stood in strong contrast to the aesthetic mood of the surrounding gallery of colonial furniture and oil paintings of well-to-do people in formal poses. *Stitching Community* was an example of exhibitioning at the ROM that did employ a collaborative approach, drawing outsiders into its planning process, and which offered accessible and involving display techniques. Consequently, the small exhibit enhanced the sensibility of the public space of the ROM.

The Institute for Contemporary Culture (ICC) departed from both the aesthetic and narrative approaches to exhibitioning in the museum. The ICC was billed as the ROM's window on contemporary society, emphasizing its explorations of art, culture, and social issues. The ICC was a favourite project of William Thorsell who saw it as 'a foil to the rest: as a statement that all of these cultures are still alive' (Thorsell, 5 November 2009).

Organizationally, the institute, according to a ROM senior manager, came under the marketing department because it is seen as 'a revenue generation thing', but it also had a Board of arts sector practitioners (Senior manager, 4 March 2009). The ROM marketing employee I interviewed was pleased with the approach taken by the ICC Board, but remarks suggest the orientation of its public approach:

Like, we always try to do something around TIFF [the Toronto Film Festival] which is what Isabella Rosellini [exhibit] was. And the year before it was the Darfur thing with the George Clooney connection ... *laughter.* God knows what we are doing this year – spring Matt Damon?

(Marketing coordinator, 4 June 2010)

Some exhibitioning fit well within the broader blockbuster emphasis of the ROM. Other exhibit ideas 'can come from anyone and anywhere. There is no one set process for how exhibitions end up approved' (ICC coordinator, 7 June 2010). Perhaps this was because of the need to be topical and relevant, but to the outside observer, appeared to reflect the whims of management. Without a collections base, and with an emphasis on 'relevance', exhibitioning at the ICC also verged into populist kitsch. The externally developed *Vanity Fair Portraits* exhibition, for example, featured celebrity photos from the magazine Vanity Fair. Event programming included An Evening with Meryl Streep, 'a personal friend of one of the Board members' (ibid.).

An example of the ICC's approach was the art installation *Housepaint: Phase II Shelter*, hosted from December 2008 to July 2009. Billed as 'the first Canadian museum to feature an exhibition focused on the subject of street art', the exhibition presented ten street artists who painted canvas houses in memory of former residents of Toronto's homeless Tent City (ROM 2007a). Programmes such as talks by a street nurse, a panel discussion on homelessness, and family activities by a street-youth organization complemented the exhibition. The canvas houses displayed in *Housepaint* were auctioned to benefit Habitat for Humanity Toronto.

Housepaint illustrated the pressures at play between social relevance and market appropriation that plagued the Institute and brings into question the 'public' functions of any exhibitioning of art. Museum attempts to achieve the position of credible social activist can be defeated by its very institutionality. Columnist Peter Goddard (2008) commented on the 'ROM-ification of street art'. Another reviewer argued that 'the effect of displaying in the soaring, cathedral space of the Crystal feels too much like the taxidermy exhibits elsewhere in the ROM. They are specimens, captured from their true habitat and placed inside the museum's hushed interior' (*The Globe and Mail*, 2008). Goddard suggested disrupting this appropriating process by instead strategically placing the works from *Housepaint* alongside the ROM's gallery displays.

In fact this did happen in a limited sense – cut-outs of homeless people carrying scrawled signs saying 'I'd rather beg than steal' and 'Stop giving handouts to the rich and start giving handouts to the poor' were placed in the ROM's lobby and outside the entrance. Street artist Dan Bergeron created the images for the Contact Photography Festival midway through the *Housepaint* show, for display throughout the streets of Toronto. Whether management recognized the irony of their placement here is unsure. But the social relevance of Bergeron's public activist art has since been challenged for its apparent marketing function: he was accused of selling out because he produced this street art as part of an advertising campaign. He now does commissions for the AGO and the ROM. The blurring between the functions of appreciating and advocating and selling was evident in this exhibitionary work.

The blockbusters – the Dead Sea Scrolls project

The final, but arguably the most important, weapon in the exhibitioning arsenal at the ROM was the blockbuster exhibition. Blockbusters are those high-budget, long-term, huge square-footage, high-volume (650 people per hour) shows for which the Garfield Weston Hall in the lower level of the Crystal was built. It was clear that major exhibitions impacted the museum significantly. They were a financially risky venture with several million-dollar budgets; they involved outside international partners, both government and other 'world-class' museums; they took a two-year lead time to prepare, and their creation and operation consumed management and operational staff almost exclusively for many months each year. The ROM's annual plan was governed by what big shows were coming (Senior manager, 1 September 2009). In the words of a ROM project manager, these larger projects took over the institution 'so that we are living and breathing that subject' (Project manager, 13 November 2009).

The RenROM redevelopment was partially premised on the economic generation of these kinds of exhibitions. Their prominence was reflected in the reorganizing of ROM's organization and operations. In the fall of 2009, the Marketing and Commercial Development department was renamed Marketing and Major Exhibitions and its director promoted to Vice President. In an all-staff memo, Thorsell endorsed the department's new strategic goals to create exhibitions that would drive attendance and revenue, and enhance marketing and public relations (Thorsell, 26 April 2010). The reorganization moved exhibit planning from a museological pursuit towards marketing and strategic relations. Blockbusters were vehicles to increase the international reputation of the ROM, to interpret important subject areas that connected to the museum's collections, and, to 'engage the world'. That marketing tagline was applied most enthusiastically to blockbuster exhibitions but in a way that distorted the line between exhibiting as something the museum always did to communicate with the public, and marketing as something the museum did for sales and business development. It was apparent that different ways of interpreting the objective of engaging the world through these large shows also connoted different attitudes towards their public function and their public nature.

The development of the major exhibition entitled 'Dead Sea Scrolls: Words that Changed the World', which ran in the Garfield Weston Hall from the end of June 2009 to January 2010, illustrates those complexities. This exhibition was planned and designed by ROM staff over a two-year period with a budget in excess of $3 million, under agreement with the Israel Antiquities Authority. The key artefacts were 16 of the iconic Dead Sea Scrolls, fragments of sacred and secular texts from about 250 B.C.E. that were buried in a cave north of the Dead Sea and rediscovered in 1947 (ROM 2009). The ROM declared that the Dead Sea Scrolls exhibit (DSS) was the most significant project in the ROM's recent history.

The Dead Sea Scrolls were iconic objects, with high recognition value, that would draw audiences: they estimated 500,000 visitors would see this show and it did attract about 331,000 in recorded attendance (Thorsell, 7 April 2010). The scrolls were also of high curatorial or knowledge-based interest – the ROM had done considerable research in this area and had a strong supporting collection, plus had already had initial discussions with the Israel Antiquities Authority, which held the scrolls. The museum took the position that the importance of the scrolls lay in their foundational role for Jewish, Christian, and Muslim religions, and their potential for inter-faith dialogue between these traditions. This, they hoped, would facilitate the visiting experiences of different cultural groups from all religious faiths, but would also aid more strategic 'community' goals of building market-oriented alliances. The topic was seen as relevant for a social forum in alignment with the agora vision and the Engage the World tagline. But further, the hope was that this type of exhibit could ensure the ROM's 'world-class' niche on the international stage, which was an academic, marketing and status-making realm occupied by only a few other museums internationally (Marketing coordinator, 4 June 2010).

The central part of the Dead Sea Scrolls project was the 17,000 square feet exhibition. The exhibit featured the scrolls in historical context, first examining life in the Jewish town of Sepphoris; Jerusalem and the Second Temple as a powerful social, political and religious centre; and Qumran, a quiet religious outpost where the scrolls were believed to have been created. The story of their discovery and subsequent conservation was prominent in the exhibit. A display of Hebrew Bibles, New Testaments and Qur'ans, together with video statements, addressed the significance of the scrolls today. The scrolls themselves were the culmination of the exhibition experience, with eight clusters of fragments displayed in a large darkened hall in specially designed cases (ROM Project Brief 2008). The museum also planned an extensive and elaborate public programme scheduled over the show's six-month tenure, with an ICC supporting exhibit, courses on religious and archaeological topics, a symposium and lecture series, three high-profile talks by controversial speakers, podcasts, educational programmes tied into the curriculum, and extensive paid special-interest tours. The three provocative lectures were scheduled just before the exhibit's opening to, in the words of the programming chief, 'upset everybody and stir it up' (Senior manager, 1 September 2009).

The DSS was to serve as exemplar for the ROM's new planning procedures for A-level temporary exhibits, and was followed by the Terracotta Warriors exhibit in 2010. The planning of this exhibition within an umbrella process that encompassed all functions within the organization was considered 'a great leap ahead on the new ROM vision' by Thorsell and senior management (DSS minutes, 5 September 2008). Planning involved senior managers with the project manager as 'the conductor of the symphony' (Project manager, 13 November 2009). The design process was closely scrutinized by the Israel Antiquities Authority (IAA), since the ROM was under contract with the IAA. The IAA had strict requirements such as number of hours the scroll fragments could be subject to lighting, even at low levels, and had final approvals of all design and written materials. The artefacts themselves were protected by the Foreign Cultural Objects Immunity from Seizure Act, which was signed off by the provincial government (Cultural Agencies, 30 April 2010).

Numerous logistical and communications problems beset the development process and the run of the show. While senior managers were in the loop, internal consultations were lacking. Workers on the front lines were poorly informed and organized. For example, one DSS volunteer remarked,

> there was supposed to be special input for this one, because this one was to be different, the whole concept was to be different because it was to involve more than just an exhibit ... They never really consulted with us very much ... However, marketing pursued its own course.
>
> (Volunteer 5, 22 October 2009)

Once installed, the exhibit experienced logistical snags and design problems such as constricted areas where people had to wait, a preponderance of text-on-the-wall, some unclear information, a lack of audio guides, and an inadequate design for tour groups. Outside the exhibit, long lines through security, confusion over timed tickets, poor handling of large groups, conflicts between user-groups, a lack of seating, and overworked volunteer tour guides could all be observed as problem areas, and visitors voiced their displeasure about this part of the experience.

As the primary tool by which the new ROM was envisioned to engage the world – and the largest project in terms of time, square footage, resources, manpower, promotion, and so on – the Dead Sea Scrolls exhibition offers a prime opportunity to inspect the ways the museum interprets its public mandate: its job and operation as a public museum. How museum management and staff interpreted 'engage the world' differed depending on how they viewed the public purpose of the exhibition – as market-oriented, scientific, social, interactive, or one other purpose not encompassed within the ROM's objectives: political. The last derives from the particular 'public interest' that sees exhibitioning as involving publics in new openness or transparency, or as addressing public issues of concern that might have a more controversial nature. Each of these perspectives on how the DSS exhibition engaged the world are analysed below in turn.

First, when engaging the public is interpreted as 'selling', success is measured by numbers of tickets sold (McLean and O'Neill 2007). While attendance was a primary reason the Dead Sea Scrolls was selected as a topic in the first place, marketing considerations also strongly shaped the form of the programming offered and all ancillary materials. As noted above, many influential senior managers had brought to the ROM corporate, business-like attitudes, market orientations, and the language of the business world. Thus, the public for them was perceived as a market, and serving publics was framed as client or customer services.

After the DSS exhibition was over, Thorsell proudly announced that group sales (package admissions and tours), had taken a lead role in 'establishing relationships with many community groups and corporations in Ontario, taking the initiative to bring visitors to the museum who would otherwise not probably attend' (Thorsell, 26 April 2010). Group sales for that fiscal year, of which Dead Sea Scrolls was the primary offering, took in double previous revenues at $1.1 million and had a 76 per cent increase in visitors (63,871 in 2009–2010). But seen from the perspective of volunteers and educators who worked on the floor, group sales created a scheduling nightmare and seriously affected the public's experiences within the exhibition. Halfway through the exhibition, one of the docents described the difficulties:

> just the other day we got an email, and they want docents for a three
> o'clock, a large three o'clock group, and then they said we've booked

now another large group for 3:30. And the person who's coordinating this wrote back saying 'well can't you make it four o'clock? Give us a chance to handle the first group.' And marketing people said 'no we can't do it. We already promised them 3:30.' 'Well why are you promising? Are you not thinking? Only about making money?'

(Volunteer 5, 22 October 2009)

This volunteer clearly blamed logistical problems on poorly thought out marketing with its emphasis on private paid tours.

The second perspective of engagement was the curatorial perspective, with its primary concern the presentation of intellectual knowledge about the scrolls. Several of the objectives presented in the design brief were scholarly, for example 'To highlight the process of scholarly inquiry and scientific discovery that reflects the ROM mission' and 'To present an exhibition that meets the scholarly standards of local and international specialists' (ROM Project Brief 2008). 'Engagement' here was an intellectual exercise: the public is presented with information that is considered scientifically important and worthy of display, and audiences emerge stimulated by and educated about the topic. But such an emphasis also has a historicizing effect – that a topic like the scrolls was something that could be distanced in the past, neutralized, and given an aura of common ancestral or universal value (Mackey 1995). This was a criticism of the ROM's curatorial perspective in the past, especially regarding the *Into the Heart of Africa* exhibit – that historicizing removed the contexts and meanings related to power and the political. The subject as presented in the DSS show was not 'difficult', that is, visitors' expectations were not challenged, and it did not elicit negative emotions (Bonnell and Simon 2007). Instead the engagement sought was the classic curatorial mode: engagement as a rational, neutral, a-political almost aesthetic exercise.

The third interpretation of 'engagement' that emerged from the Dead Sea Scrolls exhibition was intercultural. The exhibition attempted to draw out interfaith dialogue between Christian, Judaic, and Muslim religions by stressing the commonalities between traditions. In the planning process, a Community Advisory Panel of individuals of the three religions was created. As well, outreach into religious and cultural communities was undertaken to encourage attendance and cooperative programming (DSS minutes, 4 November 2008). The three-faith panel was intended 'to assist in forming partnerships, counsel the ROM on exhibition programming, and identify sources of sponsorship' (ROM 2009). But the museum was asked not to refer to them as 'community representatives' because they did not represent their entire community (DSS minutes, 25 September 2008). The co-chairs of the panel instead were high-profile local businessmen who nominally came from the three Judeo-Christian religions. In operation this was primarily a fundraising committee, with the panel supervised by the Governors' office, the fundraising arm of the museum (Senior manager, 27 May 2009). Instead of intercultural engagement interpreted as sharing in the processes of content and programme development, which the panel did to some extent, what became more important were the sponsorship opportunities. The chairs themselves donated a total of $150,000 towards the exhibition (DSS Minutes, 24 March 2009).

Thus community engagement in this instance appeared to serve a fundraising objective, more so than objectives of content collaboration or equal access or cultural sensitivity. It is unlikely that any disenfranchised agents, such as the Palestinians, would be a part of such collaboration. Engaging the public became engaging *certain* publics, those who were sources of funding or revenue, or who had some social status. Those who could afford it, such as corporate special-interest groups or donor communities, were also able to buy special access to the Dead Sea Scrolls exhibition and insider events, with invitations to participate in, and even organize, lectures on intellectual content. On the other hand, ordinary visitors, those paying $28 to get in to the museum and show, were subject to enormous line-ups with security checks of all bags, slow queues through the exhibit itself, and conflicts between user-groups on site.

A fourth area of interest was engagement interpreted as 'participation' or 'interaction' in the sense of a true agora or meeting place or 'contact zone' (Clifford 1997). While programmes like lectures and courses *were* sold out, attempts by the ROM to engage in face-to-face interactions with and among publics were limited to group and school tours, a stationary docent-in-the-gallery, and a children's activities area on the third floor. Of these, the volunteers' activities were spotty and weak, and the children's activities were embarrassingly irrelevant and difficult to find. Those people I encountered as a volunteer in the museum at the time truly wanted to share their experiences, but I was one of few staff on the ground. But if public engagement was the goal and mission of the ROM, then opportunities for some human interaction, some form of active feedback or dialogue beyond comment cards, needed to be offered. Initial suggestions in the working committee to include a space where visitors could 'share their reflections' was not followed up in the actual exhibit or in the museum (DSS minutes, 21 October 2008). In subsequent project evaluation meetings, the quality of visitor experiences and interactions was not emphasized. Discussions instead covered revenue, marketing, planning process, hardware, copyright of materials, corporate relations, and translations, while the VP of Programmes presented on 'book residuals' and 'high profile lectures' rather than public interactions.

Visitors' engagements

The important visitors' experience that emerged in the ROM's post-exhibit evaluation was 'crowding', which was treated as a logistical problem using language such as 'bottlenecks' and 'visitor flow'. But visitors' expressed engagement with the DSS exhibition did not resemble these. Most of the 11 groups who I interviewed emphasized their experiences as a spiritual pilgrimage to see venerated objects. Several expressed a heightened emotional need to 'connect with antiquity' or 'feel closer to God' or 'see it with my own eyes'. Their general willingness to talk to me and share their feelings was marked, and those I spoke to seemed to want to engage at length. Yet the museum did not offer an opportunity post-visit for face-to-face interactions with staff.

I had not expected such a high level of spiritualism in the visitors' responses, especially when compared with the languages of marketing or of scholarly inquiry employed by ROM staff and planning documents. The affective dimension was only briefly discussed in pre-exhibit planning minutes and in the Interpretation Plan, which included the aim: 'to convey the awe and the feeling of sanctity that arise in people today who are deeply affected by the Dead Sea Scrolls, particularly in people who are members of the Jewish, Christian and Muslim faiths' (DSS Interpretation Plan 2008). The interpretive aims of the exhibition were related to what the museum wanted to do, more so than what they hoped visitors would do or experience. Acknowledgement of affect took a more expedient perspective: 'The awe and mystery of the Dead Sea Scrolls and the fascinating story of where and how they were found will be key selling points in the ROM's marketing campaign' (ibid.). In all of these documents, the visitors' points of view and their experiences, particularly affective experiences, were not acknowledged as primary motivations in decision-making. Yet their perspectives were an essential element of 'engagement', and an integral part of the experience of publicness as a sharing among strangers.

Competing experiences and competing public values literally converged, on the ground, within the Dead Sea Scrolls exhibition. An incident I witnessed on 16 October 2009 illustrates this point: the Ten Commandments exhibit, put on for nine days as an add-on to the exhibition, attracted many thousands of additional visitors over the course of its showing. Confrontations between formal school tours, the marketing department's corporate tours, the roaming volunteers, and the surge of general visitors, all came together in one afternoon to create a chaos of priorities in the public space of the Dead Sea Scrolls exhibit. Tellingly, the corporate tours took precedence, the school kids were perceived as impediments and rushed through, and security staff made the tourists wait in long queues twice, both outside and inside the museum. The volunteers on duty independently chose to 'work' the lines, trying to give a personalized face to the excuses for delays, but understandably tempers were frayed. The VP of Visitor Relations would only consider this as a crowding issue saying, 'We were slammed. And we did what we could. But the team regrouped, pulled in some resources, tweaked the strategies, and Saturday and Sunday we didn't turn one person away' (Visitor Relations specialist, 27 November 2009).

Exhibitioning is political

The project manager for the exhibition was pleased with the success of the planning project and the favourable reactions to the exhibit. She said with satisfaction, 'I'll tell you how I know that people are loving it: I have not had one comment card come across my desk … which means, no one is looking for anything to change in the exhibition' (Project manager, 13 November 2009). The irony of that statement gave me pause. This was a question of scale: while the ROM might not have had visitor comment cards asking for changes, they certainly received official commentary from leaders and activist groups around the world. Just before the opening of the exhibition, Palestinian government ministers had sent letters to the ROM and the Prime Minister declaring the exhibit illegal and calling on Canada to cancel the show. Canadian activists followed up with lengthy proposals to change the content of the exhibit and texts of marketing materials (CJPME 2009). What was notable here was that the project manager considered this 'feedback' to be outside of, or not a part of, her evaluation, or at least not in the same category as comment cards.

The Dead Sea Scrolls was an example of an exhibition that was laden with convoluted political implications. The final area of 'engagement', invoking the agora, the meeting place and the contact zone concepts, all inherently involve the political. This means thinking about this exhibition beyond the scholarly topic of the scrolls as antiquities, or the frenzy of marketing for attendance, or the social inclusion exercise of inviting ethnic groups in for a feel-good session. As the *Into the Heart* controversy taught us, anything a museum does can be political; the nature of any interpretation and *exhibiting* of knowledge is political (Luke 2002). The fact that the Palestinian government ministers took advantage of the political nature of this particular museum space and topic to draw attention to their own agenda, demonstrated this. They claimed the scrolls were acquired illegally when Israel annexed East Jerusalem in 1967, thus their use in the exhibit would violate international protocols on stolen cultural objects (Ross 2009). The ROM had anticipated the possibility of controversy, but exhibitions of the scrolls in other museums had not encountered any protests (Senior manager, 27 May 2009). The Palestinian story hit the headlines globally for a few months, resulted in legal opinions, web outrage, a letter-writing campaign, on-site demonstrations, and a meeting between ROM management and a group called Canadians for Justice and Peace in the Middle East (CJPME). The Jordanian government withheld their approval of the loan of an iconic artefact, the copper scroll. The CJPME asked that the museum change the use of 'Judea' to 'West Bank'; protested the use of Hebrew place names instead of local Palestinian names; pointed out that the word 'Palestine' was never used in the exhibit text, and wanted to add the fact that the Palestine Archaeological Museum at one time housed the scrolls (CJPME 2009). The museum did not make any of the suggested changes to the exhibition, and made one correction to the website. Internally, staff were told that the 'key message' was that 'the ROM is not the forum to air these grievances' (DSS minutes, 21 April 2009). Why these nuances of language were not noticed at an earlier stage of planning is unclear. The project manager had stressed that consultation through the ROM's advisory panel, 'was a hugely important part of the project. And that is because we knew it was a political project, in terms of the Christian, Jewish, Muslim issue, and just in inherently being a project coming out of Israel' (Project manager, 13 November 2009). It appears that this consultative group, constituted in part to ensure cultural sensitivity, had not noticed these potentially volatile issues. They were again consulted when the official letter from the Palestinian government was received (DSS minutes, 21 April 2009).

The museum said they felt constrained by the IAA, which controls and lends the Dead Sea Scrolls, but also had a veto over texts and programming. Ideas for deeper engagements with political issues were discussed by ROM staff at an earlier stage (Senior manager, 27 May 2009). Undoubtedly, the IAA would never have considered the language changes demanded by Palestinian supporters.

The challenge by the Palestinians, and the role of the IAA, raises questions about the publicness of museums and about the nature of the 'engagements' we like to say we are encouraging in these institutions. Here was a real life, current example of how museums are under demand to play a role in global, cultural issues. The fact that the museum was a major cultural player in Toronto, and 'out there' with a very high media profile, made the ROM a big player as a political venue. And as with any subject connected with Israel, the scrolls' significance as symbolic icons lay beyond mere religious interpretations and intellectual debates about meaning. In effect, the IAA had the power to control this very public stage built at the ROM, but if no other dissenting voices are allowed in the museum space, can we truly say the museum is 'public'? This is not to say that the Palestinian claims were justified. But the point is that the ROM could hide as a quiet contemplative or intellectual place. The director had ruled out such an idea by continuously placing the museum in the public eye with the RenROM project. Because of the museum's 'in-public' celebrity profile, it attracted complex and political attention.

Clearly, people do not regard museums as isolated cultural spaces, or the images within them as purely historic. The ROM wanted to contribute to cultural debates, but attempted to manage them, keeping them 'historical', 'archaeological', or 'cultural', deflating present-day politics of Israel/Palestinian/Arab relations – one of the most important political crises of our age. According to one senior manager, 'we can't pretend we are not political. But we don't deal in politics at the level of … debating ownership of antiquities. There is another forum for that' (Senior manager, 27 May 2009).

The exhibit storyline relentlessly 'universalized' the significance of the scrolls as foundational to many peoples, but the Palestinians firmly re-localized the story, bringing the scrolls back into the context of their particular lives and history – a politicization of history, of heritage, of culture that is extremely complex, multivalent, and inescapable. So, should exhibits be interpreted in the context of the past, or in the context of the present? I would argue that museums now must *expect* to be used and interpreted in the context of the present *because* museums are public, and operate as media in the public sphere. Thus all types of possible present-day contexts will be brought to the table for engagement. Whether some things cannot be brought to the agora or contact zone and will not be discussed – for example debating the ownership of antiquities in an Israeli exhibit on the Dead Sea Scrolls – should itself be subject to debate and seen instead as an opportunity to explore an issue of importance to museums; perhaps even a 'teachable moment'.

The ROM's move towards 'engagement' does not appear to adequately include the public's need to know, and right to know, about the complexity and ambiguities of any cultural knowledge production. A simple example at the Dead Sea Scrolls was one visitor's demand to know 'why was my bag being checked?' Transparency about the protests, and the potential for disruption or sabotage, could have changed this moment into an opportunity for dialogue. People trust museums, and the onus is on the institution to deserve that trust by being up front and obvious about alternative claims for truth. Bob Janes (2009) has argued for the need for 'resilience', that is, being agile, adaptive and able to turn the unexpected into something positive. Building such flexibility into inflexible exhibits, and dealing productively with strongly divergent or incommensurate points of view, could be the measure of true public engagement through 'exhibitioning'.

7 Interacting

This chapter explores more dialogic and democratic possibilities for the museum in public. Inspected here is *interacting* with 'the public', a key component of the ROM's new vision of the agora. While exhibitioning with its fixed and inflexible character was less easily employed to 'engage the world', the following discussion explores those instances where the Royal Ontario Museum functioned as a more dialogic communicative interface. Exhibitioning and programming programmes at the ROM offered structured forms of public interface that emphasized communication with participants situated as audiences more than contributors; interactive or dialogic forms of media or relationships at the museum were less controlled, and more spontaneous, reactive, or open to different power arrangements.

Public programmes became the new focus of the Royal Ontario Museum in 2009. In the words of ROM director William Thorsell, the museum would be situated as a 'programming powerhouse', a new strategic direction focused on content that incorporated his ideas about the museum as an agora and would 'extend the ROM's intellectual reach under our new tagline, Engage the World' (Thorsell, 19 February 2009). These activities included all manner of informal educational programming other than exhibitioning. Interacting was sometimes a mode of communicating that occurred within mandated programming, but more frequently it was found in more informal contacts that offered important localized practices of publicness. The following analysis looks at the ways that both rational deliberative and material embodied practices were enacted here, exploring Kent and Taylor's (2002) framework of affect, intimacy, complicity, and mutuality as indicators of interactive relations. Such practices occurred *despite* the ROM's own public positioning, yet, were key to its potential renaissance as a site of more democratic publicness. This chapter asks, were there acts of interaction in the ROM's new public zones and public interfaces that breached inherent boundaries and instead built bridges through relations of engagement?

Museum volunteers provide a specific example: precarious labourers who, although often overlooked, offered everyday practices that could reflect more democratic publicness. Volunteers were neither staff nor audience and occupied an uncertain position in the minds of staff and visitors. Yet they were the ROM's primary points of face-to-face interactions with publics. They are inspected here as 'publics' offering interactive practices and sharing knowledge in ways that are seen as direct democratic practice.

Theories of 'interacting' rely on the differences between two perspectives of human communication: those of a transmissive nature, and those that are ritual in character (Carey 1989). These categories closely relate to the differences in quality between being 'in public' and being 'public'. Modes of publicness that outwardly present a fixed public face can be seen as transmissive communication, which Carey described as 'imparting, sending, transmitting or giving information to others' and 'a process whereby messages are transmitted and distributed in space for the control of distance and people' (1989: 15). The form of publicness that evokes open and interactive relations can be seen as ritual communication, which Carey defined as 'sharing, participation, association, fellowship and the possession of common faith', and a 'sacred ceremony that draws persons together in fellowship and commonality' (1989: 18). Transmissive communications imply a more fixed one-way presentation of ideas. Ritual communications invoke dialogue, social bonds, and engagement, where people do and act, rather than having things done to them. The transmissive mode of communicating inherent at the ROM underlay most of the discussions in earlier chapters. This chapter instead inspects the complex characteristics of rituality through face-to-face modes that engendered interactive and dialogic relations within the museum.

Museum programming historically was a transmissive process of communication meant to 'improve' the minds of adults and children who viewed exhibits or attended lectures or classes, a lesser adjunct to museums' central collecting and scholarly functions (Hein 1998). Later came a more nuanced understanding of the communicative experience in museum settings. Formal education programmes shifted to 'experiences' within museum environments as places of 'learning' (1998: 6). Considerable scholarly theorizing and investigation has gone into museum learning and the making of meaning (Hooper-Greenhill 1994, 1999, 2000b; Roberts 1997). Many institutions equated learning with school education programmes – a manageable compartment with proscribed teaching methods.

Museum programming is a different communicative medium than exhibitioning. Outside of museums – in historic sites, zoos, parks, and other museum-like public institutions – programming is referred to as interpretation, a term used in these institutions to describe 'any communication process designed to reveal meanings and relationships of cultural and natural heritage to the public, through first-hand involvement with an object, artifact, landscape or site' (Interpretation Canada, 1976). In studies of art galleries and public festivals, interpretive programming has been perceived as a unique communicative process situated away from representation and exhibition, and more related to artistic or expressive practices (Bourriaud 2002; Watts and Gehl 2010).

Pearson (1989) argued that organizations or institutions must consider their communicative systems as a fundamental part of ethical practice where 'interests can discover some shared ground and be transformed or transcended' (1989: 206). Ethical behaviour requires a dialogic relationship among the organization itself, its stakeholders, its users or any other interests (ibid.). This would seem to hold true especially for 'Public' institutions. Kent and Taylor (2002) argue that an ethical interactive orientation in organizations emphasizes the 'relationship': mutuality, spontaneity, empathy, a willingness to interact with individuals and publics on their own terms, and a commitment that ensures an organization gives itself over to dialogic interactions with publics (2002: 24).

These elements are well understood in museum practice and have been discussed as necessary to decentre the institution's authoritative hold as a hegemonic apparatus. This means that museums should move away from *presentation* with its implication of vested authority and knowledge boundaries, towards *exchange* using community dialogue and ongoing construction of meaning. Cases of collaboration and co-creation in museum exhibit planning have been well documented, usually invoking Clifford's 'contact zone' ideal, although the extent to which these ideals have changed practices in most museums has not been clearly demonstrated (Peers and Brown, 2003; Schorch 2013b).

Sandell and Janes dealt thoughtfully with institutional barriers to dialogue:

> Dialogue does not require that people agree with one another, but rather allows people to participate in a pool of shared meaning that can lead to aligned action … Hierarchical structures get in the way as staff attempt to navigate across and between organizational boundaries.
>
> (2007: 5)

They wrote that quality communication lies in direct human relations, openness and interconnectedness, but warned of 'all the time, energy and attention these relationships require' (2007: 11). Nina Simon observed that difficulties do not reflect a lack of desire on the part of museums, but a practical lack of organizational ability and resources (2010a: 325). Janes (2009) wrote that bottom-line thinking and just-in-time promotion of products works in opposition to the evolving, negotiated, and sustained relationship-building that dialogic interactions require. Thus, while many museums employ rhetoric of inclusion and develop programmes to promote participation and civic engagement, there is an inability to grasp what involvement and mutuality actually mean.

The qualities of dialogue ascribed by Kent and Taylor have been discussed in museum literature in relation to embodied engagements, both person to person and person to 'real things'. On a very general level, interacting in a public setting implies people communicating as social beings (Roederer and Filser 2018; Silverman 2009). Talk and passion stimulate the emotional impact of the museum encounter, experiences that could build a fundamental bond with the institution (Suchy 2006). Studies into 'affect' and heritage demonstrate that the bonds come from engagement of attention, affective connection, embodiment, and trust (e.g. Tolia-Kelly *et al.* 2017; Witcomb 2013).

Dialogue is a basic ethical position inherent in democratic publicness. The public sphere is ideally the realm of deliberation, where rational citizens come together to debate matters of concern. The formation of publics who can build and discuss knowledge is a central component of public sphere creation; the sharing of a performative space with others within an act of 'doing'. Embodiment is an important element of this, evoking an affective sense of realness, truthfulness and trustworthiness. But to find dialogue, we must find people and institutions that are open to it.

The communicative action of dialogue best occurs in 'real spaces with real people experiencing real things' (Gurian 2007). Interacting here is perceived both in terms of face-to-face relations among people, and first-hand relations with material objects. Gurian pointed to the need for interactive processes on several levels in her imagining of the museum as facilitator not instructor: organizational, mediated, and face-to-face. The first is the interactiveness of the structures and systems of the museum's organizational 'culture'; the second entails those communicative media such as digital approaches that foster interaction, and the third involves embodied experiences or first-hand dialogue. Thus 'interacting' at the ROM might be thought of in many ways: as collaborations between insiders and outsiders about plans or exhibitions; as the manipulation of digital media in exhibits or online; as sensory interactions with 'real' objects; as familial socializing among visitors; or as face-to-face conversations between staff and audiences.

The idea of material reality as 'true' – 'I saw it with my own eyes' – has historically underpinned the museum experience (Bennett 1998). The authenticity of the real thing is not only invoked by vision. It is also elicited from any embodied encounter with the material world. This can take the form of a sense of place that is emphasized in heritage research (Dicks 2000; Smith 2006), or multi-sensory experiences with artefacts or specimens. Exhibiting is itself primarily visual, but also requires bodily presence and sensations of 'being there'. Research on touch in museums has discussed the social and emotional value of object handling for therapeutic, pedagogic, and communal reasons (Chatterjee 2008).

Interactivity is also interpreted as something people do with media such as computers, where an emphasis on control and manipulation of these 'interactives' or gadgets, more than creative or emergent learning, sometimes results (Henning 2006: 89). Dicks argued that museum interactives, especially those that reproduce sensory environments, produce 'a highly elaborated, even didactic form of communication, rich with words and images, which enables quite complex and detailed stories to be told' (2003: 167). Iveson (2007), however, noted that instead of engagement, 'screens' and other media act to 'screen out' to the detriment of public life. According to Iveson, screens are more like stages in that they can be 'calculated to manipulate audiences' – 'stage-managed', as it were (2007: 210). Museum visitors also refer to this problem with media in the sense that watching screens is different and opposite to 'real' experiences, placing the onlooker in a once-removed position.

The importance of face-to-face conversations between people reoccurs in much of the museum literature on interacting. Nina Simon writes and blogs about the 'participatory museum' as an ideal museum form:

> Imagine a place where visitors and staff members share their personal interests and skills with each other. A place where each person's actions are networked with those of others into cumulative and shifting content for display, sharing, and remix. A place where people discuss the objects on display with friends and strangers, sharing diverse stories and interpretations. A place where people are invited on an ongoing basis to contribute, to collaborate, to co-create, and to co-opt the experiences and content in a designed, intentional environment. A place that gets better the more people use it.
>
> (Simon 2010b)

Simon's ideal museum of participation and dialogue involves the affective dimensions of 'intimacy' and 'complicity' that come from intimate experiences shared between strangers within museum spaces. She pointed out that such encounters generated a feeling that everyone was in the experience together although they were strangers. She felt that this museum space, a safe and neutral public sphere, enabled this complicity as 'everyone shares the excitement and energy of the show they are about to see'.

Iveson (1998) warned that such thinking might promote exclusion not participation. The difference of power between being an insider in some way, privileged to understand the rules of engagement, and being an outsider who sees this as a boundary zone, changes the nature of the public interaction. Dolan (2005) writes that such encounters of intimacy among strangers, brought on by 'doing' in public by participatory publics, must break down such power-related boundaries. True intimacy, and true complicity as a sharing among strangers, requires *risk*.

Dialogue has also been invoked as a political act, essential for communicating in the public sphere (Fraser 1992; Haugland 1996). Such a process of decision-making is highly interactive and dialogic but inevitably messy, conflictual and often irrational. The enlistment of museums as spaces of such democratic practice is widely theorized in scholarly work. On one hand scholars study institutional initiatives for governing social inclusion or citizen engagement (Newman *et al.* 2005), and at the other extreme, authors like Lynch (2014) advocate for more perilous democratic practices of 'radical trust' in museums. This kind of democratic engagement would imply commitment to mutuality and risky exchange, which would naturally involve disagreement and conflict. The idea of introducing active debate within museum spaces, ones that generate controversy and social change, is hotly argued in theory and in practice – and a question invoked by the ROM's treatment of Palestinian opposition in the Dead Sea Scrolls exhibition controversy, but also reflected by the Gaza demonstration I witnessed outside the ROM. Cameron (2013), for example, argues for the re-politicizing of museum practice away from the older neutral and pedagogic paradigm. Yet at the same time, other research has suggested that many current museum users looking for leisure or safety have no wish to see such social issues or confrontation in museums (Kelly 2003). Both arguments for and against were raised by my study participants at the ROM.

Real things and real people

The ROM museum-going experience was inherently public in an open, interactive and people-centred way: visitors do and see whatever they want in an open place for all to see, within the confines of paying their admission and staying out of behind-the-scenes areas. This interacting occurred both through first-hand experiences within the physical space or with material objects, and, as face-to-face experiences between people within that space, essential components of the museum's dialogic publicness. The new Crystal's labyrinthine floor plan, the vastness and richness of things on display, and the cacophony of peoples and voices interacting everywhere offered a sense of *uncontrolled* potential interactivity as well.

The impact of embodied presence in space was the primary level of interactiveness in the public nature of this museum. The new Crystal architecture evoked a powerful sense of place, a physical feeling of being immersed within a dramatic space. Interviewees, both visitors and workers, said that the affective sense of *occasion* experienced when entering the building was firmly embedded in their memories.

Nostalgic memories dominated this sense of occasion voiced by visitors. 'As a mom I've taken my little girl to the ROM every year, and it's a real pleasure to take her there', offered one woman. Another said

> I've had the opportunity to take my family to the ROM many, many times since our children were born. We've really enjoyed it. In fact, I was speaking to my 14-year-old son last night, who's now in grade 9 and he told me he's doing a project on the Royal Ontario Museum, at his own request.

And this testimony from another member, 'I managed to get into most of the big museums in this country and several in the States, and the ROM is just a jewel'.

One intriguing story recounted by a middle-aged woman from Montreal who was on a weekend vacation with her grown son. She was engulfed in regret that she had not been able to take the time to engage in the kind of opportunities that the museum offered.

> My son is surprising me now. I should have taken the kids to more to those kinds of places – there's some kind of regret because I see he is so interested … He wanted to come and I was so surprised – I am discovering him! It's important, I guess, things like that – we just don't take the time … Our generation, we got our kids so young and we had to work. I don't know, maybe I'm making excuses. Now my son, he's forcing my hand and I am enjoying it. I am discovering my kids over again.
>
> (Visitor interview, 1 May 2010)

This woman, a Montreal factory worker, had never visited a museum before. But her reaction epitomizes the kind of affective response to her museum visit that would gladden the heart of any museum worker. While 'knowledge' was her immediate response about the mission of the museum it also triggered a more thoughtful answer about her own life and relationships.

The positive goodwill generated suggests an underlying social mission that relates to the stewardship issues and public trust, linked to the museum as a place for nostalgia, family ties, and informal social experiences. This could be seen as a part of the 'agora' or 'engage the world' as proposed by Thorsell, and a clear indicator in the museum's social value as a public space for inward-looking, familial, affective, and emotional needs. According to Stephen Weil (1999) there is an ongoing necessity for museums to understand and communicate how they serve the public interest. Ultimately, he argues, a museum's mission must be clearly and simply linked to its public: 'If our museums are not being operated with the ultimate goal of improving the quality of people's lives, on what [other] basis might we possibly ask for public support?' (1999: 242).

Part of the undeniable sense of occasion that was stirred for people inside the museum was the affective experience offered by interactions with real objects in the museum that made knowledge tangible. Thorsell understood this powerful immediacy:

> Museums powerfully awaken our curiosity and senses to the beauties and terrors of human cultures, and the beauty and mysteries of the natural world. They do this very well precisely because most of them are filled with 'real' things, rather than images or facsimiles. It is the material nature of museums that gives them the unique power to illuminate and engage, although many museums do not use their collections to engage very well.
>
> (Personal email, 17 August 2010)

'Being in the presence of' an authentic object was a quality of publicness that was highly valued by visitors. The best examples of this feeling were expressed by those attending the Dead Sea Scrolls exhibition in the summer of 2009. Being physically close to these scroll fragments, pressing their noses to the glass, seeing and experiencing the real thing, all came up in conversation. The motivation for even coming to the exhibit was to be in the presence of the authentic object.

While Thorsell emphasized real specimens as a defining quality, in practice the sensing of those things at the ROM was limited to *viewing* those objects only – there were few opportunities in this museum for sensory experiences of touch, hearing, or smelling. Exhibits designed by Haley Sharpe tended to offer viewing from afar, as an art piece. Certain fee-based public programmes did give some stakeholders access to objects under the supervision of 'real' curators (Visitor interview, 1 December

2009). Some educators and programme staff used replicas and other props as pedagogical tools, which gave their tours a sense of material interactiveness. The Discovery Gallery and the Hands-on Biodiversity Gallery (with the Bat Cave) were two areas of the museum explicitly designed to offer more touchable, child-oriented experiences, but were older displays not part of the redevelopment project. These two interactive galleries functioned as programming spaces, animated by volunteers and some part-time staff with a tiny budget. The two galleries were the most frequented exhibit spaces in the museum, specifically because of their interactive nature (Programming worker, 19 August 2009).

Most visitors attended the ROM as a social activity or as part of a group experience (Marketing coordinator, 4 June 2010). As research has suggested, the most memorable or pedagogical museum experiences stemmed from those occasions when sociability was enhanced (Falk 2016). In one example, a ROM visitor recounted to me how the best part of his experience happened to him in the long queue threading through the Dead Sea Scrolls exhibition. A fellow-viewer took the time to explain to him how a Judaic prayer artefact worked as they shuffled past the exhibit. This led to a shared experience through the rest of the exhibition where the two strangers exchanged ideas and conversation in an extended visit that engrossed them for several hours. My informant remarked in wonder that that had been the best museum visit he had ever had.

Programming and access

While encounters between staff and visitors were limited, the effects of these moments of contact were significant. The museum employed programming department, front-of-house, and sales staff, and the department of volunteers to act as this interactive public face of the museum. Late in 2009, Thorsell presented a new strategic programming plan and department to build and professionalize a 'programming powerhouse' in the museum. This was to make the museum the 'preeminent civic forum of Toronto' and a 'powerful vehicle for communicating the stories of the ROM' (ROM Board minutes, 10 December 2009). Roughly one quarter of all ROM staff in 2009, mostly part-timers, worked in programme and educational functions, 'to enhance the exhibitions and collections of the museum' (Programmes manager, 21 June 2010). The numbers of people engaged through programming activities that year were relatively small, except for the school programme; 147,000 school children visited in organized groups while 4,250 people attended lectures, adult classes, films, and singles events, and 2,069 children attended the museum's summer camp (Royal Ontario Museum 2009: 28).

There appeared to be a discrepancy between the rhetoric employed by senior management in describing the ROM as a programming powerhouse, and the content, techniques, and objectives of what was offered on the ground. Part of this seemed to be driven by entrenched professional values, and partly it seemed to stem from the tendency to conflate programming as part of exhibitioning. Both 'programming powerhouse' as well as 'engaging the public' were interpreted as an extension of exhibitioning, organized more efficiently and more frequently around the dominant themes of major exhibitions.

The strategic plan for programmes set out in 2009 was meant to think out topics, solicit outside community ideas or recommendations from specialist staff, and analyse the kind of format or media that might be appropriate for public mediation. But a more improvised process was instead used, with senior management brainstorming generating many of the programming ideas, which were then resourced and quickly put into place. Thorsell described the evolution of a Granatstein/Landry debate on the iconic Benjamin West painting *Death of Wolfe*:

> I forget where it bubbled up. This year is the 250 anniversary of that battle, controversy in Quebec about restaging the battle. Somewhere around here the idea came, why don't we do a panel on that since we have the painting of Wolfe? Then I got, Julian and I got, a handle on it and said let's make it one of our Signature series, let's make it into a debate, let's raise it up to a really powerful level as we can.
>
> (Thorsell, 5 November 2009)

The new marketing emphasis also resulted in an increasing number of popular programmes designed as attendance generators, for example courses on body and mind healing or corporate jogging programmes. While these might be perceived as responding to the desires of visitors, the increased reliance on celebrity and gimmickry in the planning of public programmes reinforced the sense that programmes would only marginally contribute to public aims of learning, discourse, interaction or engagement. New York's Museum of Modern Art director Glenn Lowry as has been quoted as saying, 'In these difficult times, we have to hit as many buttons as we can' (Knelman 2009). The ROM had once encouraged and facilitated free admission and unstructured programming during its Friday Nights programmes, but it was disbanded and replaced with a 'Connecting Singles' programme costing in 2009 roughly $47 per event. An education employee reminisced,

> The Friday Nights, to me, used to be the one night when it wouldn't be a sea of white faces. Do you know what I mean? This was Toronto

at its best. There used to be multi-generational families that would come – I am talking about grandparents, parents, the kids, nephews. And the beautiful thing was watching the children explaining the arte-facts to their parents, their grandparents. I mean, this is real learning ... I really felt like I was a part of something important when I was working on Friday nights. I don't feel the same kind of community connections that used to be there. I don't feel the same kind of people have access anymore.

(Education worker, 10 June 2009)

Accessibility was singled out as an important goal under the new program-ming strategy, clearly an essential aspect determining the publicness of the museum. Access was defined in policy as 'the ROM's responsibility to make its collections, information, programs and services physically and intellectually available to ROM employees, volunteers, and members of the public'. The policy set out details for three areas of access, intellectual, physical, and use of public areas. The ROM has been recognized by the Ontario government for its leadership in providing accessibility through Renaissance ROM and subsequent initiatives (Thorsell, 16 December 2009). The focus of their access initiative was tactile tours offered for people with visual impairments and sign language tours for those with hearing impairments, developed in conjunction with outside professionals, but conducted by trained volunteers.

Access for 'communities' through programming also received signi-ficant attention, specified in policy as serving community groups and mini-mizing cultural barriers (ROM Board of Trustees 2010). One curatorial employee from a visible minority pointed out there was a tendency to view access as an issue of attendance or physical entry, but that for multicultural audiences, 'the *visibility* of a particular culture as a *living* culture was an important part of the public face of that culture, which the museum should support' (Curator C, 15 June 2010). To help social inclusion goals, the ROM made serious attempts to diversify programmes, and developed cul-tural diversity staff training programmes.

Access can also not just be equated with physical entry or even enabling inclusion, but as the ability to 'engage'. Thorsell himself com-mented that access was 'Not just getting into the doors; it's access to the experience' (Thorsell, 5 November 2009). Jennifer Barrett (2011) cri-tiqued the ways that museums assume that they are 'public' institutions and therefore accessible. She wrote that access means a sense of *owner-ship* by the public, of knowledge production and dissemination. The implication for museum programming is the essential need for interactive participation in order to engender ownership and true accessibility. The

ROM appeared to have a long way to go before its programmes would achieve this level of access and engagement. But the museum did hire an audience development specialist who began to develop strong programmes to deal with racialized thought and language within museum structures, and think about ways that groups could take on programme creation and dissemination.

Interacting through client services

The most basic of face-to-face exchanges occurred at the ROM in mundane situations: the 'front-of-house' activities, using the museum's parlance, which included ticket-sellers, security guards, and people soliciting memberships. While not normally thought of as 'public' functions in a knowledge-building sense, as most businesses recognize, these are the front-line workers in customer service who contribute to the clients' or visitors' immediate impressions about an institution. They provided an obvious public function in orienting visitors, serving basic needs, and projecting an official presence in all spaces of the ROM. And in many cases, these workers also acted as unofficial informational and even educational staff, telling stories about the building, the objects, the history and anything else people asked them. The communicative interactions involved face-to-face encounters and exchanges, where first impressions were important, contacts were embodied, and perceptions tended to be more affective.

On the other hand, these staff could be seen to effectively manage the public interactions within the building. They were the gatekeepers who decided who entered or not. They directed traffic along desired flows and restrained publics who might want to be noisy or unruly or dared to touch the objects. They recited acceptable information and stories that had been vetted by management. They presented a well-planned, highly manipulated public face that schooled people in how to be visitors – how to have an ideal visitor experience in a museum-like manner within the walls of the ROM. Thus, the public nature of 'interacting' within these front-of-house operations can also be seen less as attempts at openness or reducing interpersonal and organizational barriers, and more as an attempt to regulate the 'in-public' behaviours of the visiting public. This stems from the perception that these were *managed* relationships: publics were clients thus subject to practices and structuring logics of customer service professionals within a rubric of the 'visitor experience' (Senior manager, 27 November 2009). Museums increasingly foreground experiences as what visitors can get out of their visits; but such experiences can also be used as a form of control or presented as a commodity to be acquired. The marketing-oriented motivation for this at the ROM was clear (Visitor relations specialist, 20 May 2010).

The tone of the interacting through this public face of the museum was often blatantly sales-oriented. Front-of-house staff members were responsible for 'proactive sales' where once they were merely ticket-takers (Senior manager, 27 November 2009). Thus, the first real person a visitor interacted with in the museum would try to sell them a membership. The visitor must have come away with the sense that this public space was a store, entered through an exchange of funds, and from which they must obtain some kind of valuable asset. This shift to a marketing/client services focus for the visitor experience front-of-house group occurred during the RenROM development. The same interviewee described the conceptualizing of client services staff as revenue-generators as a 'pretty fundamental shift of how the organization has changed'. Previously, until 2001, 'visitor experience' was a department that encompassed the ROM's *educational* experiences. The innovation under Thorsell was to compact and compartmentalize the title 'visitor experience' into a group responsible for any 'client' services. Thorsell's 'Engage the World' vision was framed by the visitor experience group as a business orientation that would drive their face-to-face contacts within a marketing perspective: finding out 'what the audience wants in terms of product and services' and ensuring that the museum responded accordingly (Visitor relations specialist, 20 May 2010).

Programming and education staff did not share the client-oriented perspective. One suggested filling the museum's spaces with animators and performative interactions. Another employee offered this suggestion:

> I think in some senses, maybe if there was $280 million spent on the Crystal, it would have been nice to have said, 'let's put enough in our bank account so we can have a member of staff in every gallery'. Because it doesn't take a lot – 'hey this is a shark' – to make the experience memorable.
>
> (Programming worker, 19 August 2009)

An exhibition planner summed up these conflicting orientations to 'interacting':

> It's as if people are going to walk in the doors of a museum, purchase a piece of museum as a consumer transaction, and walk out again. That's not what museums are for. It's about participation and enhancement and enrichment of people's lives.
>
> (Exhibit planner, 11 December 2009)

Interacting through volunteers

The ROM has relied on the Department of Museum Volunteers (DMV) throughout its history to take on the museum's 'public face' duties, including leading tours inside and outside the museum, assisting education and programming, taking on a range of logistical and assistive tasks, and informally helping visitors on the museum floor. The museum's first Members Volunteer Committee was established in 1957 when a group of female museum members offered to help curators with collections (ROM 2007b). More specifically, the museum didn't have enough people to dust the huge Chinese collection (Volunteer 1, 23 April 2009). The women, of course, were looking for more than household work; they wanted to learn something (ibid.). The ROM welcomed the services of these women in a support role – working with collections, organizing fundraising events, and assisting educational activities. According to Hooper-Greenhill and Chadwick (1985) such helpers, by virtue of their sex and their ancillary tasks, were marginalized within the museum world in general. Orr wrote that since volunteering was seen as a replacement for real work, or as 'better than doing nothing', this implied 'that it was not useful or of a lower hierarchy' (2006: 198). Gray and McColl pointed out a similar attitude towards front-line workers expressed by 'those people up in the offices' in their study of museum bureaucracies (2018: 128).

Volunteers might be thought of as boundary objects: they are neither staff nor audience; neither insider nor outsider; they are not knowledge experts but not total amateurs. They occupy an ambivalent position in the minds of staff, in the minds of visitors, and in their *own* minds (Stebbins 1996). They straddle and bridge the transmissive/dialogic communicative divide in the types of programming they do but also in their personal status as independent non-staff who offer non-professionalized understandings of museum content. Yet, and perhaps because of their in-between position, at the ROM they were called on to bridge the museum and the outside world as the museum's primary points of real contact. The museum could not undertake many of its core functions without these people, particularly those activities involving interactions with the public (DMV president, 6 March 2009). Holmes found in her study of museums in the US and Canada that 'to the visitor, the volunteer *is* the museum' – the face and the voice of museum knowledge (2003: 242). To ROM visitors, the volunteers and client services were *the* public interface of the museum. The public do not differentiate between staff and volunteer when they enter the ROM. What a curious thing, that an organization devoted to publicness as their mandate would depend on marginalized volunteer labour to be their first line of interactive contact.

Volunteers, however, were consistently marginalized by ROM staff, patronized in a gendered way as 'just' the volunteers, or even as 'feisty busy-bodies' (Senior manager, 29 April 2009). The volunteers' knowledge was perceived as amateur, as not central to the real workings of the museum. One senior manager voiced about the DMV, 'it's almost like a parallel universe, isn't it?' (Senior manager, 1 September 2009). Orr has studied the 'them and us' relationship between volunteers and professional staff in museums, noting that 'the professionals have an elite status as those who have the knowledge and expertise, and volunteers entering this social world are dependent on them to provide information' (2006: 204). The president of the volunteers at the ROM acknowledged the 'we/they' scenario that resulted in trouble getting information:

> they tend to, the ROM, operate in their own world in a way, and I have difficulty getting information that I need sometimes. Because they are working in their own little group and they don't always think to include us. And I am trying to make them aware.
>
> (DMV President, 6 March 2009)

Within the strategic engagement initiatives during RenROM this tension worsened. The volunteer corps was increasingly constrained to perform as understudy, and they felt they were forgotten by management. Volunteers who were interviewed were concerned that in the new bottom-line mentality that emerged during RenROM, interpretive experiences within the museum were being reoriented as a product sold through the marketing department and cheaply staffed by part-timers. They perceived that corporate group tours initiated by marketing were taking over the public presence of the ROM, the visible face-to-face interactions. As one volunteer guide expressed it, 'that's always been our province, in terms of doing the tours ... People were really demoralized and depressed here because we felt we were being marginalized' (Volunteer 2, 27 April 2009).

But because their function was not prioritized in the museum, and not under institutional scrutiny, volunteers were also avenues for alternative knowledge-creation. This was not entirely evident at first analysis: the touring and teaching style employed by many docents tended to lecturing. But there was a radical element in the knowledge-building by these people. Their place on the front line in close contact with visitors gave them immediacy, interactiveness, and, if they chose, the freedom to engage with visitors in ways that were not controlled.

In this space of face-to-face engagement with the public, knowledge-creation became dialogic and performative. So, while much of the guided tours and formal programmes offered by volunteers followed institution scripts, a great deal of it did *not*. A long-time docent described her relationship to publics on her tours:

> We're the story tellers. We're the keepers of the flame, more or less. We tell the stories of this place, and we pass the stories on to the next generation of docents, or meeters and greeters, or gallery interpreters. And the people who come in want to hear the stories. People love gossip, so you tell all the gossipy little bits about the collections. You don't necessarily have to tell them that this [*totem pole*] was raised in 1870 and it's made of red fir or Douglas fir. Who cares? They want to know that one person was supposed to be swallowed by the totem pole, swallowed by a fish ... I tell stories because the public wants to hear the stories. And that is an age-old tradition, coming from the oral traditions of the earliest, earliest tribes 10,000 years ago ... And that's what a museum is supposed to do.
>
> (Volunteer 2, 27 April 2009)

The forms of pedagogy by such amateurs were complicated tactics that blended 'craft' practice, exchange, social relations and intimacy. Any of these communicative characteristics bring the volunteer/visitor engagement into a more radical dimension. Such behaviour could be seen as micro-tactics through which individuals unconsciously challenge rigid structures of institutions and assert autonomy, even unintentionally (de Certeau 2002).

The craft practice of the volunteers entailed telling stories about their relationship to objects, and back and forth exchanges of knowledge with people. And in this process, knowledge was created and co-produced through social relationships:

> Part of the process is not just learning the official information, but also around that ... One of the objects I am dealing with is a lump of gold ore. So I walk around whatever gallery and show people this lump of gold ore ... So in the process of this I learned about some of the crazy characters involved in gold exploration, how gold mines are described, how they are financed ... and I engage people who turn out to be former miners or mineralogists in some conversation, so I could then learn some more about it.
>
> (Volunteer 3, 4 May 2009)

This volunteer reflected the inherent the sociability of his position, the relationship-building with other people in the museum public, combined with a passion for learning and excitement about interacting within the

knowledge-rich environment of the ROM. Each volunteer who was interviewed expressed passion, love, and loyalty about the collections, the
museum as an entity, and their role as public 'explainers'. The same volunteer was adamant that 'really the most important thing that we do is to
engage people'. Engaging others in what they themselves take pleasure in
was repeated by many volunteers, and most felt their public role in doing
that 'made all the difference in the world' (Volunteer 4, 9 May 2009).

Their interactions with visitors had a performative aspect – the idea that
they gained affirmation from people when they shared their knowledge
and passion 'in public' – as well as a sense of mutuality, complicity, and
even intimacy in some cases. Intimacy took the communicative transaction
past teaching, even past dialogue and deliberation, into a familial space.
This closeness was a step past social interaction and occurred through
affective appeals to personal experiences such as favourite topics, or memories of past visits as a child. Visitors were invited to come into the
museum space as if into the volunteers' private living rooms to see special
things. This involved an embodied closeness to real things and real people
in an inspiring public setting (Gurian 2007).

People responded to those invitations especially if it resonated with
their own personal experiences. I observed as well a tendency of some visitors to want to enter those more intimate spaces and strike up personal
conversations (where are you from? do you go to school? do you have
kids?) and relay their private thoughts (my grandmother had one of those,
I worked in that area, I hate what they did). Audiences appeared willing to
develop those relations and exchanges with volunteers because of their
non-threatening demeanour, or perhaps their perceived amateur status – an
exchange as among equals where both sides offer experiences and knowledge. The volunteer was then seen as not staff and not necessarily
authoritative, but as an insider or as a bridge to the inside, and privy to
behind-the-scenes knowledge. This was also a kind of 'performative
encounter' as articulated by Kanngieser (2013), possible because of the
ambivalent subjectivity of the volunteers: both sides are able to bypass the
constraints of pre-established subject positions. Some audience members
reacted with hesitation or some with scorn to anecdotal and familiar pedagogical styles. But in the best volunteer-led experiences, groups of visitors become small publics, briefly bonded by their interactions with
instructor, space, and performative encounters. These were the museum
experiences they likely will remember.

While it might be useful to see volunteers themselves as a unique form
of audience – members of 'the public' who used the museum sphere as a
higher level of identity-production – they were also active producers of
knowledge, not only for their own meaning-making but by others. They

were consumers but they were also producers; they were visitors and yet form part of the visitor experience for other visitors. And because they were neither insider nor outsider, they were also connectors and bridges, occupants of a public sphere that is both boundary zone and contact zone.

Such groups must also be viewed as 'publics', possessing a more vigorous sense of community not only for identity-construction, but sharing their knowledge as a form of democratic practice (Simon and Ashley 2010). This constitutes 'world-making' in Arendt's sense, that fundamental understanding of publicness and political life (the sharing of power/knowledge), which involves actively coming together in dialogue or argument, for better or worse, around shared matters of concern (Kanngieser 2013). Michael Warner has said 'the world made in public action is not an intended or designed world, but one disclosed in practice' (Jagose 2000). While micro in scale, the genuine connection fostered between some volunteers and some publics at the ROM was creative and constructive for those participating, and for the institution itself. In those moments of public contact an affective bond formed that was often cited by staff, other volunteers, and some visitors as the reason they loved the museum and continued to return. And this generative sense was cited as something museum management wanted to attain, through both the visions of 'agora' and 'engagement'.

When the institutional interest in public programming as the 'new vision' for the ROM was developed in 2009, it placed the activities of the DMV under the scrutiny of museum management. This drew the volunteers into an increased emphasis on marketing. Some in the DMV saw this as an unprecedented acknowledgement of the volunteers' important role (DMV president, 10 May 2010), while others complained that this inflicted marketizing strategies of the museum on their generosity (Volunteer 6, 6 May 2009). DMV guides were, for the first time, asked to lead money-generating corporate and group tours – volunteers were leading for-profit programmes. Their gift of labour was being sold in order to help the museum economically and to enhance the visiting experiences of private sector customers. The implication in the minds of some volunteers and some staff was that there had been a shift in corporate culture. It framed the museum 'agora' not as a forum for dialogue, but more as a market-place for selling goods and services – a creeping privatization of public services.

The institutionalizing of their labour potentially affected the freedom and alterity of the volunteer corps, especially the social, performative, and conversational nature of their volunteering. However, as Renaissance architecture, galleries, and marketing projected a 'new global vision' for the ROM, old and nostalgic visions continued to be relayed through their tours and public encounters. As aesthetic exhibits and digital interfaces were installed, embodied social exchanges using creaky carts full of objects were still offered within those antiseptic surroundings. And as some managers desired to take advantage of volunteer guides to lead corporate tours, use of these unpaid workers was sometimes as reliable and feasible as 'herding cats' to quote a group sales manager – they resisted institutionalization. If Louise must take Friday off to go to the doctor, well, the museum will need to find someone else. These responses do not represent a concerted plan or consistent actions, but were emergent, intermittent, and inconsistent responses to institutionalizing and marketizing processes that just do not sit well with these older, perhaps wiser, amateur workers. And as the museum slowly withdrew some of the status and insider perks that these volunteers once prized (like taxi chits and multiple entry into limited exhibitions), the resistance (some say stubbornness) of a few increased.

The experiences and relationships of the volunteer corps during Renaissance ROM could serve as an instructive model of the kind of interacting the museum might want with people in the outside world. These were important localized, dialogic practices that occurred despite the museum's efforts, not because of them, yet were key to the ROM's potential performance as a site of cultural democratic publicness. Such a perspective on the nature of its publicness takes advantage of an existing desire by communities to treat 'their' museum as an integral (not instrumental) democratic space within society, and museum-making as a social process of knowledge-building and relationship-building.

Boundaries and bridges

The kind of investment of self which some people were willing to commit to this public space – volunteers and others like the museum educators and the Friends member I interviewed – bespoke the potential of 'interacting' as a beneficial type of publicness. But there were two kinds of interacting evident here, one that was managed or mediatized, and one that was more open and dialogic. Employing one or the other was sometimes an indication of motivation: to join a club in order to impose boundaries, or, to activate a public to invest in a fundamental purpose. One is safer, easier and less of a commitment, and the other is full of risk and exposure and even intimacy. One a boundary zone, one a bridge or contact zone.

The director maintained he was engaging with the risky style of interactions at the ROM. He was quoted in an Ottawa newspaper as saying 'museums aren't stentorian, standing up and just telling you the way the world is. There's more room for debate and different points of view'

(Deachman 2010). But he also said in an interview for this research, 'I always make a distinction between productive controversy and destructive controversy. Productive controversy is a good thing' and referred to the high-profile debate on The Death of Wolfe and the Battle of the Plains of Abraham as an example of good controversy. Evidently, the fact that the museum set the agenda, the location, the debaters, and the moderator was seen as a good way to manage 'unproductive' controversy. 'That is not a passive role – it's a much more activist one' he said. The museum seemed prepared to take an active stance in areas that were less controversial, and consequently less risky, for example on environmental issues.

The ROM was taking measured steps in its entry into issues of concern. How to deal with unscheduled flare-ups of debate and engagement was not addressed, as the Dead Sea Scroll controversy showed. But whether actions like photos of homeless people in the boundary zone around the museum translated into active debate was questionable. A volunteer relayed a story of two tours he witnessed in the local neighbourhood, one led by the ROM workers and the other by an outside group:

> The ROM tour is about 'here is the church and here is what happened' … and there are graves all around the church, about 6000 people there around the church. So OK, that's the ROM tour. The other tour talked about the graves and how the indigenous buried their dead and what it meant to be an archaeologist digging up graves of indigenous people versus whites – and this should not be done. Here is a particular group with a different social agenda. Should the ROM take that approach? My feeling is that it should be more like the second tour. That there ought to be some sort of addressing of controversial social issues – forget about controversial, even just social issues around these things. But then you run into problems of ideology and problems of individual perspectives and there is no way to control that. And because you are a public institution you have to back right off of that. While these other folks, what do they care? … For an institution to address that? Are you going to try to *influence* social policy or are you going to merely *study* social policy?
>
> (Volunteer 3, 4 May 2009)

The astute volunteer understood that the assumption of an activist role in the public sphere was fraught with risk, but his gut feeling was that the 'second' tour was the right one.

Thus, how to define 'engagement' continued to be a problem within the ROM. If seen as an interactive and dialogic process, then there was little evidence that the organization was re-aligning its underlying assumptions and practices. A 'visitor experience' staff member said:

> The reality is, public trust, public institution, most of what we see in any city, town, country, where they have landmarks, is owned by the public. So if the public doesn't feel a connection to it, there's something wrong in terms of you're missing the mark, in terms of delivering on whatever the promise tends to be. But I mean that there's a real acceptance here at the ROM, that Engage the World is an absolute must, we must engage our constituency. Has to do with relevancy, has to do with even respect for your mandate. Ultimately a lot of mandates and missions are created and they're very lofty usually. But to what end do people go to, to actually make sure that those are actually meaningful? I think that one of the interesting things about Renaissance ROM is that it has actually aligned the 'speak' to the 'action'.
>
> (Visitor relations specialist, 20 May 2010)

The boundary I felt between what 'real' people did outside, and the activities of people inside, was an artificial boundary where the museum's 'action' did not address 'speak', contrary to the opinion of that visitor relations specialist. The rhetoric was there, but not the action. The museum had constructed this boundary because it feared the painfulness and the confrontation of the real spilling inside. But if the place was going to live up to its 'public' potential then it needed those spontaneous face-to-face encounters where people are not afraid to put aside their fears and act honestly. Then people will be eager to make an investment in the museum. Certain people do, like the volunteers, whose passion for place was evident. The ROM could have been an important spot in the public realm for people to actively invest their senses of ownership and know that here was a site where they could come to seek understanding, connection, commitment, mutuality, closeness, propinquity, empathy, risk, and commitment (Kent and Taylor 2002).

Part III
Revisioning

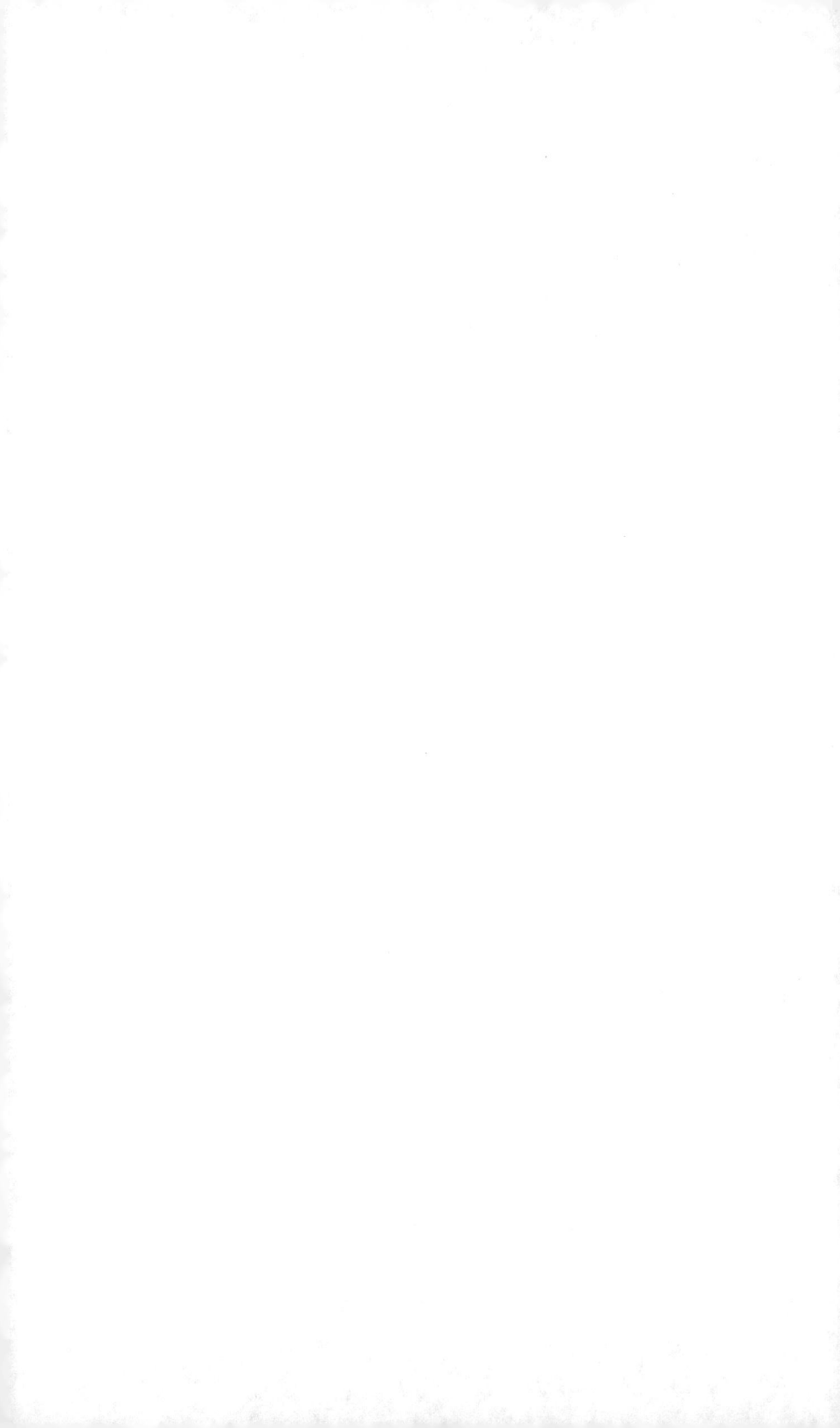

8   Revisioning publicness at
the ROM

The Royal Ontario Museum was evidently not a simple public institution
that provided a service to publics. Competing interests resulted in multiple
and sometimes conflicting ideas about the purpose of the museum, who it
served or maintained relations with, organizational and infrastructural
issues, its corporate communicative positioning, and its visitor-oriented
public interfaces. All of these contributed to multiple manifestations of
publicness at the ROM. This chapter reviews the nuances and complica-
tions to the word 'public' that became evident during this research, then
concludes with a discussion of the important types of publicness that have
emerged, whether this reflects a change or renaissance, and the extent to
which new museology principles are, or might be, performed at the
museum. It suggests how changes in publicness have strong implications
for the future role of museums such as the ROM as 'public' institutions in
our society.

Public sphere

The clearest invocation of the publicness of the museum was spatial. The
ROM was an extraordinary location with striking old and new buildings,
enabling a sense of 'being there' that came from its volumes, its displays,
and its crowds. While aesthetically the RenROM's public space was
described as alienating or disorienting, and the old areas as too stuffy, the
place-ness of this sense of publicness was undeniable. There had been a
physical renaissance: a makeover, a new public face. This challenged the
professional habits of many of the museum staff, requiring that they innovate – not a bad thing. But by the end of William Thorsell's tenure in
August 2010 it appeared that the museum had not found a way to move
past its brash new public face to offer something deeper inside. The new
galleries of objects were a clue to this failure: row upon row of beautiful
things to passively admire, 'wallpaper' on architectural walls.

It was also evident that the ROM continued as a bounded sphere in the public realm. The museum renaissance did not bring about a new public sphere in a Habermasian sense as a space where publics come together to express, debate, and negotiate relationships and common concerns. The agora concept invoked by Thorsell had all the characteristics of civic space, but the rhetoric did not match the practices: the museum was not a public space encouraging the entry and participation of any and all. A combination of traditional programming like lectures and new popular programmes like corporate jogging did not engender a sense of public deliberation. Nor did the museum's exhibiting styles that were predominantly aesthetic, blockbuster, or kitschy. On a fundamental level the expensive ticket price made the ROM only a partial public sphere, accessible to a percentage of the public who chose to pay, and useable only in ways determined by the institution. Although the museum's 'access' strategy did offset entrance fees with some free or cheaper access times, it confined certain social and ethnic visitors to limited times and offerings.

The public

'The public' for the ROM did not radically change as a result of the renaissance development, except in one small respect: its enlargement to include more ethnic communities. The museum continued to privilege people with money – sponsors, patrons, paying corporations, members, even volunteers. This had the effect of emphasizing difference and status hierarchies, not cooperation and democratizing. Senior management were elated about high-profile events, elite attendees and the success of the Governors in raising so much money for the RenROM project. But the favouring of elites resulted in complaints about high admission and about museum spaces blocked off for private functions. The 'public' was thought of as patron or audience or client, in all cases people targeted with institutional selling more so than knowledge-building dialogue or collaboration.

Such praise of high-priced donors as the primary public was not new at the ROM, but a continuation and even strengthening of a long-standing tradition. What was new was the ethnicity of those patrons, perhaps signifying the new Toronto. 'Communities', a code word for ethnic groups, began to embrace the museum as their public space as well. Attracting ethnic or minority community members became a major thrust during RenROM, partly to raise sponsorship dollars (such as the large investment made by Michael Lee-Chin to build the Crystal), partly to grow their audience base, and partly to open their doors to those people who made up the majority of Toronto's population. This public, whether patron or audience, tended to be drawn from the elite ranks of these cultural groups. For their part, cultural groups were eager to assert their newfound abilities and resources to acquire cultural capital in Toronto society through the museum, as well as enjoy its interesting public space.

Institution of public government

Informants routinely responded to the question 'how is the museum public?' with the answer that the ROM was a 'Public institution'. That the museum acted on people's behalf as a representative of government and the public trust seemed obvious to them. But what the trust was, and how the institution served the 'public interest' was difficult for some to probe further. Most employees articulated the public trust in terms of what the museum already did and what their jobs already were. Education, steward-ship, and research were common responses to the public service provided. These reinforced the idea of publics as audiences or receivers of informa-tion and services, and 'Public institutions' as places that act on their behalf rather than sites of democratic action in the public sphere.

Within the museum, ideas about the 'public trust' were subject to some tension between research/collection and public/education, which streamed down to affect many aspects of the ROM's public interfaces. Curatorial pursuits appeared to have organizational weight and institutional inertia that supported that claim of public purpose. There appeared to be an under-lying objective to separate or protect the research function from 'the public', and to regulate the nature of the information disseminated to publics. There was a curatorial reluctance to engage in a public intellectual role except under the controlled environment of exhibition and lecture. Yet, education came across as an important public trust for visitors and within the institution on a policy level. The museum was positioned fore-most as an education institution in its Vision statement: 'The ROM will inspire wonder and build understanding of human cultures and the natural world.' Education and programme staff and front-line workers, as well as visitors, were equally persuasive that education was the core job of the museum as a 'Public institution'.

New managerial objectives during the RenROM period, however, inter-fered with both the curatorial and education emphases. Public purpose was increasingly aligned with audience development and marketing. By 2009 education and exhibition were situated by management as part of strategic marketing. Thus it appeared that the traditional shape of 'Public institu-tion' at the ROM, as a service dedicated to research or education or stew-ardship, was being challenged by outside economic forces of the 'private' world.

Public/private

The apparent debasement of the 'public service' functions of research and education to encroaching business and management mentalities reflecting private enterprise attitudes was an underlying concern for many of the workers and volunteers interviewed. The loss of public space and services to investing stakeholders or activities for profit was evident in branding, marketing, and sales initiatives in the museum. Most ROM management and staff referenced the overwhelming pressure to increase revenue as a major issue at the museum. How to pay for the RenROM redevelopment and how to maintain debts and operating expenses were at the forefront of the minds of staff. Fundraising and marketing had assumed a huge place in all institutional activities, and marketing became a central driver in planning any public interfaces. Management spoke about the necessity of the business perspective and bottom-line thinking. The public value of communicative efforts on all levels shifted from the *process* of relationship-building, to *products* for sale and consumption.

Workers at lower levels indicated that demands to maximize programming that was profitable influenced the conditions of their work and the kinds of programmes offered. The drive to cut costs and to market the museum was cited by curators as disruptive, or resulting in poor exhibition design with no evaluation. Some of the resistance to the RenROM development and to attendance-generation efforts came from insiders and visitors who wanted to retain the old and dowdy 'public service' flavour of the museum, however unprofitable. An ongoing sense of conflict between public and private value was manifest in several ways, including a fight for space on the museum floor. Private group programmes such as private tours and corporate entertainment activities took precedence in scheduling, use of space, and in 'presence' within galleries. The common thread was the perceived incursion of private demarcation into public shared space.

Visitors complained about the increased marketization on several counts. The largest concern was the high cost of tickets. The second was the disruption of their visit and free use of space by special and private functions, especially in the face of the admission price.

Openness

Operating an organization in a public manner also requires a publicness that implies informational transparency and openness, exposing ideas or activities to public scrutiny for truthfulness or credibility, or even debate of ideas. But openness and transparency was instead discussed at the ROM in terms of 'access'. This word was initially used by Thorsell to indicate physical, sensual, and intellectual access to collections. But the museum was not an institution to easily open itself to outsiders and relinquish communicative control, even though this is necessary for true transparency. The museum was a highly managed bureaucracy, without the kinds of procedures needed to ensure openness. The desire to control information seemed to emerge from the lack of will of bureaucracy, but also from the museum's historic role as authority and gatekeeper of knowledge, and from the power exercised by the director. The inability to be public in the sense of transparency and openness resulted in one-way forms of communication of information, where public contacts were controlled, information dispersed either top-down or inside to outside, authority rested at the top of the organizational hierarchy, and some voices were privileged over others.

On an intellectual level, the museum's preoccupation with knowledge control, and the status and authority presumed by the possession of expertise, also lay behind its lack of openness. The internal weighting of curatorial activities, and even the positioning emphasizing international research as a distinctive mark of the ROM, had a boundary effect. The positioning closed the museum off from external, less scholarly knowledge-building, deemed as 'public' education. The internal emphasis that scholarly pursuits were separate from public interaction, rather than an important *part of* public sphere processes, resulted in the situating of the public interfaces of exhibition and programming as intellectual dissemination more so than opportunities for open debate.

The concept of the agora implies openness to dialogue and debate. All levels of staff voiced interest in active participation and social relevancy in their public services. But after the arrival of William Thorsell there was a sense of nervousness about collaborative knowledge processes. Instead, public consultations with outside groups became processes for market analyses and fundraising activities, or were regulated into focus groups that did not have substantive input into the content of exhibits and programmes. The lack of visibility about the behind-the-scenes knowledge production calls into question how contents and meaning were constructed. The design of the RenROM galleries was an example of a process that lacked transparency, not only for outside publics but for most staff members as well: very few curators had input into designs; authority rested with an upper executive; few decisions and approvals were discussed by staff; co-creation with outside groups was non-existent; and exhibits were not subject to evaluations.

Publics formation

Such closed boundaries of engagement were inherent, assumed, and adopted by most ROM insiders, but also by most visitors. There was no sense among visitors interviewed that they should have any role in the construction of the knowledge presented there, and most appeared satisfied with being communicated *to*, rather than discussed *with*. But public, democratic culture is based on the principles of equality of participants, accessibility, and deliberation on the common good. Thorsell's vision was that this kind of coming together and engagement would result from the kind of architectural, gallery, and strategic programming development that occurred with the museum's redevelopment: that the creation of an agora within a beautiful envelope, a meeting place for all cultures, would allow the museum to engage the world. The new ROM was instead a beautiful space that *discouraged* social engagement, to paraphrase Thorsell's agora speech.

Social engagement did emerge, however, within the informal and spontaneous actions of people within the space: for example, by visitors within their first-hand, embodied experiences in the museum, and by volunteers acting as autonomous agents in relation to the visitors they encountered. The interestedness, the attention, the motivation required to form a public of shared interest did exist there. Some visitors spoke of childhood memories, about warm reactions to family socializing in the ROM, or awe-inspiring moments that came from being in the space itself, or from encounters with people or objects. It was from these reactions that a different sense of the importance of the museum came to the fore – an unmanaged, affective sense that linked to concepts of public trust and stewardship and communal sociability but in a less-defined mode: a 'being' public. This sense of 'being there' – of exposure to real things, of conversation with social groups or sometimes with staff – gave visitors a sensibility that perhaps the museum did intend. This occurred in non-institutionalized, in-between places: in the hands-on activity galleries; in the chaos of March Break where kids and parents raced around and did what they wanted; in the pandemonium that characterized once-free Friday nights. These random and unplanned activities seemed to offer more of a contact zone of sharing and creative-making. Sharing knowledge and passion between strangers through creative 'doing' is the very essence of public formation and world creation. This clearly happened on occasion in informal programmes and interactions with and among volunteers and some educators wherein strangers came together and produced something new.

New museology and social change

Whether these kinds of engagements can be considered deliberative in the democratic sense of the public sphere is another question. These were affective encounters, but they did not necessarily discuss matters related to the common good or contribute to social transformation. For the museum to act as an agent of social relevance or democratic practice (two essential ingredients of 'new museology') would require deliberate actions or facilitation of others to engage in dialogue, debate, or disagreement. The museum and Thorsell felt that those kinds of deliberations occurred within their formalized programmes, 'engaging the world' with the kinds of debates that occurred during lectures or exhibitionary activities.

But facilitating dialogue, debate, or disagreement must be more than a boastful claim. There must be a sense of public ownership of the debate, and some kind of social benefit. Thorsell wanted to take an activist role, but differentiated between 'productive controversy and destructive controversy' that would be allowed in the museum. Such a distinction is difficult to square with the complicated process of democratic debate. The museum wanted to contribute to cultural debates, but attempted to manage them, keeping them historical or cultural, deflating the *political*. Understanding how to house the open-endedness and riskiness of debate, rather than an 'in-public' *display* of engagement-like situations, is difficult for any public institution. But the new museological notion of museums as agents of social change, as well as Clifford's idea of the 'contact zone', are characterized by that danger. Such a contact zone was not evident in the ROM's exhibits and programmes, or in its other communicative initiatives, or in the organization's own systems and practices. It is questionable whether relevance and risk is even possible within an 'institution', especially one compromised by a marketing orientation.

'In public'

Commentators in the Toronto media were inclined to assess Thorsell's activities at the museum as showmanship – a position more about 'putting on view' than a suggestion of 'let's talk'. As Message (2006b) pointed out, one version of new museology is about the desire to project an image of newness, of global relevance and of postmodernity through big-money renovations. Attracting public notice, of celebrity, is a form of publicness that invokes a performance of status and the putting on of a public face. It is likely that the ROM's rhetoric about controversy and relevance reflected a need to make an appearance 'in public' in a way that would garner attention.

A prominent 'in-public' performance was the ROM's ongoing 'world-class' rhetoric during RenROM. This language was echoed in all levels of corporate governance ('The ROM will be a world leader in communicating its research and collections') and patronage ('support a great spectrum of Arts and Science from around the world!'), communications ('Engage the World'), programmes ('Dead Sea Scrolls: Words that Changed the World') and operations (foreign government-level negotiations for Terra Cotta Warriors and Dead Sea Scrolls). The language of 'world class' permeated the media and government discourses about the museum and economic development, and the attitudes of many day-to-day visitors to the museum. It demonstrated the desire and positioning undertaken to situate the museum on an international scale.

The new Crystal was clearly situated in the perspective of management, staff, and those external to the institution as a catalyst to attract attention, generate patrons and attendance, and induce new ways of thinking about the ROM. But as many critics pointed out, envisioning the Crystal as the main attraction of the ROM was not the way to develop meaningful connections with people or revision the place of the museum in society. Despite the large investment of resources and attention in the RenROM project, staff, visitors, and non-visitors pointed out that it was not very people-friendly and had numerous difficulties as a museological space.

The ROM succeeded in creating a new crystal face to display for world attention, a publicness that demonstrated its wealth and relevance in a celebratory fashion. The conceptualizing of the new museum as 'hardware' induced the sense that the museum was an aesthetic icon for consumption, or a tourism destination where one could say 'I've seen it', or a sensational piece of 'bling' as one viewer described it. Thorsell and the ROM created a 'celebrity publicness', combining corporate communicating and pedagogical exhibiting to draw the attention to the museum as a consumable 'landscape of desire'. In place of a deliberative public sphere, a mediated celebrity publicness bestowed visibility and credibility through 'in-public' performance. Here, celebrity-tinged exhibits like Darfur at the ICC, with huge images of refugee children projected on the Crystal, played out political issues on a stage, replacing real debate of issues. In that case, seeing and being seen trumped negotiation and relationship-building as the means used to build public knowledge about matters of concern.

Museum renaissance?

The old ROM, pre-renaissance, was a troubled, inward-looking institution, at the service of a small segment of the population, and conflicted in its public role. The boundaries around the museum were far more evident than the bridges. Did this renovated museum change that condition?

I did feel a new sense of publicness in my intensive study of the ROM, but not the kind I was seeking. My concern that emerged from the Gaza protest witnessed outside was the way the museum built fences to protect its temple inside. The new ROM had appeared to break down the barricades with its architectural collision, and had verbally acknowledged a desire to act as a public sphere in the classic sense. But it was hard to understand where the agora was located, except in the corporate language. Were the queues outside the special exhibitions what Thorsell meant by an agora? Were the new memberships sold to ethnic community members considered to be the agora? Were the polite crowds at the Death of Wolfe lecture considered to be the agora? Was the agora located in the cocktail event for Royal Patrons in the C-5 lounge? I looked for an agora that was a 'contact zone', a site for drawing together, negotiating, and bridging among those inside and those outside the museum. But the museum had not become what it had promised.

The ROM that I studied for this book was deeply divided between rhetoric and action. What the museum said was not what they did on the ground. While its corporate communicative positioning spoke of agora and public engagement, its actions in practice drew on its historic roots, preoccupations, and methods. The 'public interest' articulated and carried out internally perpetuated professional concerns with research or conservation or the next exhibition or school programmes or educational activities. 'Publicness' in its richest sense of the common good, of dialogic relationships, of open democratic practice, was not a concern of museum management and was only sensed by some employees and volunteers who worked day-to-day with publics in the museum. The ROM appeared unable or unconvinced of the need to move from control and authority in its treatment of knowledge and information, towards mutuality and sharing required by the concepts of agora or engagement.

This divide is the very essence of an 'in-public' style of publicness. While Thorsell cultivated a public face of relevance, contemporarity, and engagement, this was not manifest behind the scenes. The talk *about* the museum as radical and sometimes controversial, and the erection of an expensive building that symbolized this pose, was 'publicness' at the ROM in a new form. Here lies the renaissance at the ROM: an acknowledgement of the importance of publicness and the creation of a new public sensibility, but one which is about 'in publicness', or the performance of celebrity.

Celebrity publicness, in a way, protected the museum inside from the authority-challenging, unmanaged nature of democratic publicness. It seemed as if Thorsell understood that the public world had to be acknow-ledged, but still wanted to control the mode of entry. The museum pre-RenROM was disparaged as dusty and insular, with cultural boundaries built to exclude. The new ROM met the criticism head on, but got lost in the publicity. This was a hollow pose, with galleries and public pro-grammes that did not live up to their impressive billing. Because the celeb-rity pose was superficial, however, basic questions remained: in this performance of publicness, did public discussion really change? If what was accomplished inside the museum had not really altered, how was this museum truly relevant? What was the social benefit of having this museum?

This book took an institutional perspective, asking how the ROM was situating *itself* as a public institution operating in the public interest. It appeared at first glance that what was important here were the three internal, and warring, concerns: curatorial/research, education/public, and marketing/money. But these instrumental concerns reflected the 'how' of the organization rather than the 'why'. To reach into the 'why' of the operation – the underlying assumptions that society, as well as the museum, made about its purpose as a Public institution – required a deeper and more subjective investigation. To what extent the ROM's public inter-faces achieved their purpose, according to perceptions of its public interest, was a question that required an examination of the museum's rhetoric and its actions on the ground, but also an inspection of outsiders' perceptions and my own critical observations. Publics and non-institutional players appeared to have different interests than management and employees. Publics demonstrated their wishes to use this Public institution for leisure or entertainment, education or self-improvement, and status-enhancement, and also had sentimental notions about identity-formation. Thus on a basic level, there was a disconnect and a barrier between institutional interests and practices, and the lives and concerns of people for whom this public museum existed.

For my part, I was searching for evidence that the publicness offered here had democratic potential; that the agora of the rhetoric was enacted on the ground in a contact zone that broke down the kinds of boundaries I perceived around the museum. This was a principle of new museology: that museums act as agents for social change. But while the rhetoric indi-cated the ROM fully supported this goal, there was little evidence of it in practice. I was interested in speculating how the protest I saw outside the museum might have evolved if participants had the ability to include the public space of the ROM in their performance. But inside the ROM the sensation that one was protected from the realities of the outside world was still very strong.

New museology particularly argues that access to museums be broadened to include all members of society. The ROM had taken steps to promote social inclusion, but only in strategic ways emphasizing class privilege. Measures were needed to level up the unequal power relations to change the museum into a cultural commons, an open part of the public realm.

What would it take, on the ground, to assure the operation of the ROM, and museums like it, as socially relevant spaces and processes in the public sphere? The commons, and the contact zone, are difficult places to operate. They require balancing the tensions inherent in the public realm, acknowledging the multiplicity of demands and players, and coming up with creative ways to offer openness, engagement and negotiation at the same time as specialization, difference and argument. The museum during its renaissance did not have the organizational strength to take on that kind of commitment.

Removing the boundaries would be an important first step. This is the essence of 'publicness'. The boundaries I perceived at the ROM were not only between insiders and outsiders, but within the institution between words and action, and management and workers. The divide between words and action has been argued here as a case of 'in publicness', the construction of a rhetorical face that belies real practices in the museum. Constructing a celebrity persona was a questionable tactic that served short-term goals that would not sustain long-term support and buy-in from the society within which the ROM was embedded. Closing the disconnect between words and deeds would be a first objective. Building sustainable, dialogic public relationships – not just words, symbols, or products for consumption – would be the goal.

Removing the boundaries within the organization would be another necessary step. My study found multiple differences in goals and public sensibilities within this single museum. A strong hierarchy reinforced these divisions. Power relations do not facilitate knowledge construction. Sharing authority and building consensus might require admitting that the museum was itself multiple, contingent, and divided. A flatter organization, a release of control and professional restrictions, and taking the time to negotiate goals and processes could result in a renewed sense of place and purpose within broader society.

The boundary I perceived between inside and outside would be the most difficult obstacle to address. Finding a means to overcome the financial barriers in a broad and equitable way was essential. But removing the intellectual barrier between inside and out, the habits of authority and control, was a significant issue that had long been discussed with little impact at the ROM. It was as if those exhibits that line the museum walls acted as a boundary between insiders and outsiders: on one side of the designer gallery spaces was a range of people, issues, conditions, and real objects, and on the other an equally multifaceted crowd of viewers, wanting to experience and contribute to the inside complexity. Bringing down the wall between inside and out would require opening up to local knowledge-making, making sure people have a stake in the institution, committing the time to seek out external contacts, developing ethical public relations, and taking the risk that conflicts, mistakes, and defeats might be the result.

Building bridges across the boundary zone has been a specialty of volunteers at the museum, born from their marginality and independence within the museum space. Here are ordinary people whose broad access to behind-the-scenes excitement and interactions led to the development of passion and commitment. This relationship could serve as an instructive model of the kind of connections the ROM might want to propose to more people in the outside world. In a way, this takes advantage of an existing desire on the part of many members of the public to just 'be there' within the museum public space *as if* they belonged there. Such an experience could be seen in the faces of visitors who remained in the central Currelly Gallery, just sitting, not attending or reading. It was an affective, even numinous, immersion that can build bridges between publics. Professionals inside might think about the way that facilitating such experiences, contributing to the capacity of others for affective and intellectual experiences, might be an ethical and rewarding practice.

Finally, building in the flexibility and resilience to break down those boundaries requires understanding, connection, commitment, mutuality, intimacy, and risk, all facets of dialogic communication. Being able to respond quickly and openly to an event like a protest on the steps of the museum would require an investment of time and acknowledgement of vulnerability. What was exciting about being in the midst of that Gaza event was the riveting sense of complexity and risk, both facets of transformative learning. This was an 'in-public' moment, but not one that emphasized consumption or status-enhancement in the manner of celebrity 'in publicness'. Instead, there was a feeling of importance, of 'occasion' and of revolution, since anything could have happened. Bringing that sense *into* the ROM should be a goal.

Other museums in public

While the setting for this study has been a single museum operating in a Canadian context, these challenges faced by the Royal Ontario Museum are shared internationally. All museums must consider why and how they exist in the public interest, their relationships with publics and stakeholders, and the transparency of their activities. Sandell and Nightingale have eloquently called for all museums to counter inequalities and engender social justice, but admit this role remains 'largely untapped' (2012: 2). Missing from many introspections is analysis of the publicness of decision makers and decision-making, no matter how much goodwill is devoted by museum professionals to diversifying workforce or audiences. Collaboration and inclusion are still unequal if boundaries remain in who holds power – between insiders and outsiders, words and action, and management and workers.

The challenges of publicness have to be met differently within different scales of museums. The ROM considers itself a universal museum, in league with the British Museum, and receives no funding from the national government. Thus it does not bear the pressure to represent collective narratives of a unitary nation-state, nor is it called upon to be a window for the world to look in on the nation – both characteristics of national institutions of public government. Pressures on national museums to balance these two remits, inward responsive and outward illustrative, can test their organizational systems and practices. When Te Papa Tongarewa in New Zealand developed in the 1980s and 1990s, scholars applauded its new organizing, collecting, and relationship-building that promoted indigenous Maori agency, as well as the ways it played a part in altering the national narrative towards biculturalism (Dibley 2007; Message 2006b). With the twentieth anniversary of Te Papa in 2018, Chief Executive Geraint Martin's words on the museum's website reflect the 'public' pulls on these types of museums: 'Our aim is that every New Zealander can see themselves reflected at Te Papa, and that international visitors can understand the richness and diversity of Aotearoa.' The National Museums in Canada – a cluster devoted to history, art, science, and natural history in capital city Ottawa, with others across the country – also bears this mandate of serving a national public, promoting publicness in operations and ownership, transparency, taking risks, and ensuring that equality drives the construction of an 'authentic' national public profile. Ruth Phillips has long explored how curatorial practices in Canada's national museums have taken steps to bridge boundaries with indigenous as well as immigrant communities in these operations (e.g. 2003, 2018).

As a universal style of museum, The ROM instead might be compared to the British Museum. The discourse around the status of universal museums posits that they should orient themselves towards a global public more so than a local or national museum. Neil MacGregor (2009), director of the British Museum, talked about positioning that museum as 'the private collection of every citizen in the world'. Deriving power and agency from their historical associations with the state, this positioning reinforces their ability to play on the world political stage as state-like operators, more so than building bridges with publics. The nature of their publicness and public accountability is not easily investigated. Gray points out that, although public governments provide legislative frameworks for universal museums (e.g. British Museum Act of 1753), 'there is little in the way of direct, hands-on, control by central government of the detailed day-to-day functioning of these institutions' (Gray 2008: 214). Thus public accountability could be a key question of publicness in relation to international universal-style museums.

Interestingly, the British Museum has been called out expressly for its behaviour in the public interest, particularly its ethics and lack of accountability, but also for its internal operations. In all of these cases, it has been younger generation activists who have sought to use the British Museum's prominent in-public position to press for broad societal changes, and they have done this within the museum's walls. Youthful activists have kept the pressure on the museum over its imperial-era collection practices as an important ethical issue in the public nature of museums (Procter 2019). Other protests have repeatedly tackled the British Museum's sponsorship policies, targeting, for example, their acceptance of the oil company BP's sponsorship funding for a major exhibition on Iraq, and for BP's role in climate change (Busby 2019). Taking public issues of concern into the museum, by outside interest groups, are acts of citizenship expressed at an everyday, bottom-up level. They parallel the Gaza protest I witnessed at the ROM, but actually take those public issues into the inner sanctum to confront museum management.

Equally interesting is the work in breaking down boundaries taken by practitioners themselves, significantly also led by youthful workers. Museum Detox in the UK, for example, is an affiliation of Black and minority ethnic museum workers whose aim is to rock the system they work within. They represent at conferences and activities within the sector but also outside the museum discipline to 'campaign, lobby, debate, advocate' as they say on their website. Their White Privilege Test confronts museum leadership and employees to self-scrutinize in a transparent, in-public way. These activities and the British Museum protests share not only the age of the campaigners, but the fact that challenges are coming from outside or below the established professional and management players and systems.

Youth and grassroots pressures have not yet been shown to bring actual changes to how large universal and national museums act in the public interest and deploy clarity and accountability in their practices. But a final example of new ways of being that are affecting museums internationally lies in the emergent role of city museums. This is a scale where museums have managed to respond to local and everyday matters of concern in transparent ways that give agency and ownership to diverse publics, and embody Kent and Taylor's public relationship indicators (2002). Larger museums might have trouble with moving the weights of their histories and bureaucracy into a 'public' mode. But city institutions can be nimbler. The work of the Museum of Copenhagen, for example, has been brought forward as an exemplar of strong practices. Parby argues that fluidity and transition is the norm in cities, not the exception (McCarthy *et al.* 2013). Museum of Copenhagen can mobilize a whole museum with local residents and practitioners to tackle public issues in a way that draws the whole institution into a city-wide dialogue with political impacts (Parby 2015). In Canada, the Museum of Vancouver has developed similar innovative practices where public relationships are foregrounded in the development of multifaceted media and programmes, both inside and outside the museum's walls. It is revealing to compare the publicness of practices and relationships in the ROM – a universal, but sometimes perceived as a city, museum – with the Museum of Vancouver. The MOV's soul-searching in 2007 – at the same time the ROM was in the throes of revisioning – involved complex consultations and relationship-building with the museum's city (Gosselin 2014). Their exhibition Sex Talk In The City of 2013 is an exemplar of publicness in museum practice. Curator Viviane Gosselin writes how 'interdisciplinarity, intense levels of collaboration and elements inspired by a pedagogy of historical thinking were strategies deployed to create unconventional clusters of ideas about sexuality'. The entire museum and multiple of elements in the population of Vancouver were transformed for two years in a consultation process that must be seen as a true 'public sphere'. That intense process of engagement before the exhibitioning was as equally important as the final exhibit itself, removing boundaries on multiple fronts.

The core reason for undertaking this project was to think critically about why museums exist and what they are supposed to be doing for whom. The future of museums must be pursued in the context of making a difference to people's lives, not for the mere purposes of ensuring the survival of the museum with its traditional activities and behaviours. Thinking about the ROM as a 'public' institution at this important point of 'renaissance' was meant to shed some light on whether such museums might serve as ethical agents of social change and whether this was a reasonable goal. Museums need something other than showmanship and celebrity publicness. If they are to be valued public institutions worthy of support, public dialogues about our world need to take place within their public sphere, however defined. This requires breaking down boundaries around their walls and within their walls, and facilitating publics that want to be inspired by, connected to, and involved in, their public knowledge work. And it might require that risk and resilience be an integral part of their public nature.

References

Abram, Ruth J. (2007) Kitchen Conversations: Democracy in Action at the Lower East Side Tenement Museum, *The Public Historian*, 29(1), 59–76.

Abt, Jeffrey (2006) The Origins of the Public Museum, in Sharon Macdonald (ed.), *A Companion to Museum Studies* (pp. 15–34). Oxford: Blackwell Publishers.

Adorno, Theodor and Max Horkheimer (2000) The Culture Industry: Enlightenment as Mass Deception, in Simon During (ed.), *The Cultural Studies Reader*, 2nd edn (pp. 31–41). London: Routledge.

Althusser, Louis (1971) Ideology and Ideological State Apparatuses, in Louis Althusser (ed.), *Lenin and Philosophy and Other Essays*. New York: Monthly Review Press.

Anderson, Benedict (1983) *Imagined Communities: Reflections on the Growth and Spread of Nationalism*. New York and London: Verso.

Anderson, Gail (ed.) (2004) *Reinventing the Museum: Historical & Contemporary Perspectives on the Paradigm Shift*. Walnut Creek, CA: AltaMira Press.

Angus, Ian (2001) *Emergent Publics*. Winnipeg: Arbeiter Ring Publishing.

Arendt, Hannah (1998 [1958]) *The Human Condition*, 2nd edn. Chicago, IL: University of Chicago Press.

Ashley, Susan (2005) State Authority and the Public Sphere: Ideas on the Changing Role of Museums as a Canadian Social Institution, *Museum and Society*, 3(1), 5–17.

Ashley, Susan (2010) Vision, Translation, Rhetoric: Constructing Heritage in Museum Exhibitions, in P. Burns, J. Lester, and L. Biddings (eds), *Tourism and Visual Culture, Volume 2: Methods and Cases*. Wallingford: CABI.

Bailkin, Jordanna (2002) Radical Conservations: The Problem with the London Museum, *Radical History Review*, 84(Fall), 43–76.

Barnett, Robert (2003) [Powerpoint presentation], ROM, 14 May.

Barrett, Jennifer (2011) *Museums and the Public Sphere*. Oxford: Wiley-Blackwell.

Belfiore, Eleonora (2018) Whose Cultural Value? Representation, Power and Creative Industries, *International Journal of Cultural Policy*, 1–15.

Bennett, Tony (1995) *The Birth of the Museum: History, Theory, Politics*. London and New York: Routledge.

Bennett, Tony (1998) Pedagogic Objects, Clean Eyes, and Popular Instruction: On Sensory Regimes and Museum Didactics, *Configurations*, 6(3), 345–371.

Bennett, Tony (2006) Exhibition, Difference and the Logic of Culture, in I. Karp, C.A. Kratz, L. Szwaja, and T. Ybarra-Frausto (eds), *Museum Frictions: Public Cultures/Global Transformations* (pp. 47–69). Durham, NC: Duke University Press.

Bernard, Paul (1999) Social Cohesion: A Dialectique Critique of a Quasi-Concept. Strategic Research and Analysis Report, Department of Canadian Heritage.

Boast, Robin (2011) Neocolonial Collaboration: Museum Contact Zone, *Museum Anthropology*, 34(1), 56–70.

Bonnell, Jennifer and Roger I. Simon (2007) 'Difficult' Exhibitions and Intimate Encounters, *Museum and Society*, 5, 65–85.

Bourdieu, Pierre (1984) *Distinction: A Social Critique of Taste*, Richard Nice (trans.). Cambridge, MA: Harvard University Press.

Bourdieu, Pierre (1990) *The Logic of Practice*. Stanford, CA: Stanford University Press.

Bourdieu, Pierre (1993) *The Field of Cultural Production*. New York: Columbia University Press.

Bourdieu, Pierre and Alain Darbel (1991) Conclusion, Caroline Beattie and Nick Merriman (trans.), *The Love of Art: European Art Museums and their Public* (pp. 108–113). Cambridge: Polity.

Bourdieu, Pierre and Loïc Wacquant (1992) *An Invitation to Reflexive Sociology.* Chicago, IL: The University of Chicago Press.

Bourriaud, Nicolas (2002) *Relational Aesthetics*, Simon Pleasance and Fronza Woods (trans.). Dijon: Presses du reel.

Bradshaw, James (2010) Ten Years, One Huge Crystal, Zero Regrets, *The Globe and Mail*, 21 August, pg. R3.

Browne, Kelvin (2008) *Bold Visions: The Architecture of the Royal Ontario Museum*. Toronto: ROM.

Busby, Mattha (2019) Campaigners Protest against BP Sponsorship of British Museum, *Guardian*, 16 February. Accessed 17 February 2019 at www.theguardian.com/culture/2019/feb/16/campaigners-protest-against-bp-sponsorship-of-british-museum.

Butler, Shelley Ruth (1999) *Contested Representations: Revisiting into the Heart of Africa*. Toronto: Broadview Press.

Butler, Shelley Ruth (2010) Stitching Community: African Canadian Quilts from Southern Ontario Until 6 September 2010, Royal Ontario Museum, Unpublished Exhibition Review, 9 July.

Butler, Shelley Ruth and Erica Lehrer (eds) (2016) *Curatorial Dreams: Critics Imagine Exhibitions*. Montreal: McGill-Queen's Press-MQUP.

Calhoun, Craig (2005) Rethinking the Public Sphere, Presentation to the Ford Foundation, 7 February. Accessed 2 January 2019 at www.researchgate.net/publication/228513835_Rethinking_the_Public_Sphere.

Calhoun, Craig (2006) The University and the Public Good, *Thesis Eleven*, 84(February), 7–43.

Calhoun, Craig (2015) Forward, in Caroline W. Lee, Michael McQuarrie, and Edward T. Walker (eds), *Democratizing Inequalities: Dilemmas of the New Public Participation*. New York: NYU Press.

Cameron, Fiona (2003) Transcending Fear – Engaging Emotions and Opinion – A Case for Museums in the 21st Century, *Open Museum Journal*, 6 September [online]. Accessed 6 July 2006 at http://archive.amol.org.au/craft/omjournal/ archives.asp.

Cameron, Fiona (2006) Beyond Surface Representations: Museums, 'Edgy' Topics, Civic Responsibilities and Modes of Engagement, *Open Museum Journal*, 8 (August) [online]. Accessed 15 March 2018 at http://pandora.nla.gov. au/pan/10293/20061101-0000/www.amol.org.au/omj/volume8/volume8_index. html.

Cameron, Fiona (2013) The Liquid Museum: New Institutional Ontologies for a Complex, Uncertain World, in A. Witcomb and K. Message (eds), *The International Handbooks of Museum Studies, Volume 1* (pp. 345–361). Chichester: John Wiley & Sons.

Capra, Fritjof (2004) *The Hidden Connections: A Science for Sustainable Living.* New York: Anchor Books, Random House.

Carey, James W. (1989) A Cultural Approach to Communication, in *Communication as Culture: Essays on Media and Society* (pp. 13–36). Boston, MA: Unwin Hyman.

Casey, Dawn (2002) Museum Leadership: Good Management, Good Judgement [podcast], Museum of New Zealand. Accessed 23 June 2018 at www.r2.co. nz/20021024/.

Chatterjee, Helen J. (ed.) (2008) *Touch in Museums: Policy and Practice in Object Handling.* Oxford and New York: Berg.

Cheney, George and Karen Lee Ashcraft (2007) Considering 'The Professional' in Communication Studies: Implications for Theory and Research Within and Beyond the Boundaries of Organizational Communication, *Communication Theory*, 17(2), 146–175.

Cheney, Terry (2002) The Presence of Museums in the Lives of Canadians, 1971–1998: What Might Have Been and What Has Been, *Cultural Trends*, 12(48), 37–67.

Chong, Derrick (2007) The Rise and Rise of Art Museum Marketing, in Ruth Rentschler and Anne-Marie Hede (eds), *Museum Marketing: Competing in the Global Marketplace* (pp. 203–214). Amsterdam: Elsevier.

CJPME (2009) CJPME Analysis: Changes for the ROM Dead Sea Scrolls Exhibit. Montreal: Canadians for Justice and Peace in the Middle East.

Clifford, James (1997) Museums as Contact Zones, in James Clifford (ed.), *Routes: Travel and Translation in the Late Twentieth Century* (pp. 188–219). Cambridge, MA: Harvard University Press.

Coombe, Rosemary (1991–1992) Author/izing the Celebrity: Publicity Rights, Postmodern Politics, and Unauthorized Genders, *Cardozo Arts & Entertainment*, 10, 365–395.

Coombes, Annie E. and Ruth B. Phillips (2015) Museums in Transformation: Dynamics of Democratization and Decolonization, in Sharon Macdonald *et al.* (eds), *The International Handbooks of Museum Studies, Volume 4* (pp. xxxiii–lxiii). Chichester: Wiley-Blackwell.

Couldry, Nick (2003) *Media Rituals: A Critical Approach.* London and New York: Routledge.

Coxall, Helen (1997) Speaking Other Voices, in Eilean Hooper-Greenhill (ed.), *Cultural Diversity: Developing Museum Audiences in Britain.* London and Washington, DC: Leicester University Press.

Currelly, Charles Trick (1976 [1956]) *I Brought the Ages Home.* Toronto: Royal Ontario Museum.

Cutlip, Scott M., Allen Center, and Glen Broom (2000) *Effective Public Relations.* Englewood Cliffs, NJ: Prentice-Hall.

Davies, Sue (2008) Stakeholder Engagement in Publicly Funded Museums: Outlining the Theoretical Context and a Proposal for Future Research. Accessed 26 August 2018 at https://culturalpolicyjournal.files.wordpress.com/2011/05/sue-davies-july 2008.pdf.

Deachman, Bruce (2010) The Museum Reinvented the Exhibits, *The Ottawa Citizen*, 18 May, E1.

Dean, David (2009) Museums as Conflict Zones: The Canadian War Museum and Bomber Command, *Museum and Society*, 7(1), 1–15.

Debord, Guy (1971) *La société du spectacle: la théorie situationniste*. Paris: Buchet.

De Certeau, Michel (2002) *The Practice of Everyday Life.* Thousand Oaks, CA: Sage Publications.

Dewdney, Christopher (2008) Crystal Blurs ROM's Natural Wonders, *The Toronto Star*, 5 July, p. ID06.

Dewey, John (1946 [1927]) *The Public and its Problems.* Chicago, IL: Gateway.

Dibley, Ben (2007) Antipodean Aesthetics, Public Policy and the Museum: Te Papa, for Example, *Cultural Studies Review*, 13(1), 129–149.

Dicks, Bella (2000) *Heritage, Place and Community.* Cardiff: University of Wales Press.

Dicks, Bella (2003) *Culture on Display: The Production of Contemporary Visitability.* Maidenhead, Berkshire: Open University Press.

Dolan, Jill (2005) *Utopia in Performance: Finding Hope at the Theater.* Ann Arbor, MI: University of Michigan Press.

Duffy, Dennis (2006) Triangulating the ROM, *Journal of Canadian Studies*, 40(1), 157–181.

Duncan, Carol (1995) *Civilizing Rituals: Inside Public Art Museums.* London: Routledge.

Ellsworth, Elizabeth (2002) The U.S. Holocaust Museum as a Scene of Pedagogical Address, *Symploke*, 10(1–2), 13–31.

Falk, John H. (2016) *Identity and the Museum Visitor Experience.* London and New York: Routledge.

Flynn, T., Fran Gregory, and Jean Valin (2008) Defining Public Relations [online]. Accessed 28 February 2010 at http://publicrelationsincanada.blogspot.com/2008/12/defining-public-relations.html.

Foucault, Michel (1991) Governmentality, in Graham Burchell, Colin Gordon, and Peter Miller (eds), *The Foucault Effect: Studies in Governmentality* (pp. 87–104). Chicago, IL: University of Chicago Press.

Fraser, Nancy (1992) Rethinking the Public Sphere: A Contribution to the Critique of Actually Existing Democracy, in Craig Calhoun (ed.), *Habermas and the Public Sphere* (pp. 109–142). Cambridge, MA: MIT Press.

Fraser, Nancy (2005) Mapping the Feminist Imagination: From Redistribution to Recognition to Representation, *Constellations*, 12(3), 295–307.

Gilmore, Abigail and Ruth Rentschler (2002) Changes in Museum Management: A Custodial or Marketing Emphasis?, *Journal of Management Development*, 21(10), 745–760.

Giroux, Henry (2004) Public Pedagogy and the Politics of Neo-liberalism: Making the Political More Pedagogical, *Policy Futures for Education*, 2(3&4), 294–503.

Goddard, Peter (2008) Takin' it from the Streets, *The Toronto Star*, 14 December, p. E10.

Gosselin, Viviane (2014) Civic Museography, Porous Narratives, and the Choir Effect: Sex Talk in the City at the Museum of Vancouver, *THEMA. La revue des Musées de la civilization*, (1), 107–115.

Gosselin, Viviane and Phaedra Livingstone (eds) (2016) *Museums and the Past: Constructing Historical Consciousness*. Vancouver: UBC Press.

Gramsci, Antonio (2005) *Selections from the Prison Notebooks*, Quintin Hoare and G.N. Smith (eds and trans.). New York: International Publishers.

Gray, Clive (2008) Instrumental Policies: Causes, Consequences, Museums and Galleries, *Cultural Trends*, 17(4), 209–222.

Gray, Clive (2017) Local Government and the Arts Revisited, *Local Government Studies*, 43(3), 315–322.

Gray, Clive and Vikki McCall (2018) Analysing the Adjectival Museum: Exploring the Bureaucratic Nature of Museums and the Implications for Researchers and the Research Process, *Museum & Society*, 16(July, 2), 124–137.

Grenoways, Hugh and Lynne Ireland (2003) *Museum Administration: An Introduction*. Walnut Creek, CA: AltaMira Press.

Gurian, Elaine Heumann (2007) Introducing the Blue Ocean Museum: An Imagined Museum of the Nearly Immediate Future, Keynote speech, ICOM 2007 Conference, Vienna, Austria, 19 August.

Habermas, Jürgen (1984) *The Theory of Communicative Action: Reason and the Rationalisation of Society, Volume 2*. Boston, MA: Beacon Press.

Habermas, Jürgen (1991) *The Structural Transformation of the Public Sphere: An Inquiry into a Category of Bourgeois Society*, Thomas Burger (trans.). Cambridge, MA: The MIT Press.

Hall, Stuart (1997) *Representation: Cultural Representations and Signifying Practices*. London: Sage Publications.

Hannay, Alastair (2005) *On the Public*. London: Routledge.

Haugland, Ann (1996) Public Relations Theory and Democratic Theory, *The Public*, 3(4), 15–25.

Hein, George (1998) *Learning in the Museum*. London and New York: Routledge.

Hein, Hilda (2006) *Public Art: Thinking Museums Differently*. New York: Rowman Altamira.

Henning, Michelle (2006) *Museums, Media and Cultural Theory*. Maidenhead: Open University Press.

High, Steven (2009) Sharing Authority: An Introduction, *Journal of Canadian Studies • Revue d'études canadiennes*, 43(1), 12–34.

Holden, John (2006) *Cultural Value and the Crisis of Legitimacy*. London: Demos.

Holmes, Kirsten (2003) Volunteers in the Heritage Sector: A Neglected Audience? *International Journal of Heritage Studies*, 9(4), 341–355.

Hooper-Greenhill, Eilean (1994) *Museums and Their Visitors*. London and New York: Routledge.

Hooper-Greenhill, Eilean (1999) Education, Communication and Interpretation: Towards a Critical Pedagogy in Museums, in E. Hooper-Greenhill (ed.), *The Educational Role of the Museum*, 2nd edn (pp. 3–27). London and New York: Routledge.

Hooper-Greenhill, Eilean (2000a) *Museums and the Interpretation of Visual Culture*. London: Routledge.

Hooper-Greenhill, Eilean (2000b) Changing Values in the Art Museum: Rethinking Communication and Learning, *International Journal of Heritage Studies*, 6(1), 9–31.

Hooper-Greenhill, Eilean (2003 [1992]) *Museums and the Shaping of Knowledge*. London and New York: Routledge.

Hooper-Greenhill, Eilean and A. Chadwick (1985) Volunteers in Museums and Galleries: A Discussion of Some of the Issues, *Museums Journal*, 84(4), 177–178.

Hudson, Anna (2006) New! Improved! The Rhetoric of Relevancy in a Construction Boom, *MUSE*, 24(3), 38–41.

Hume, Christopher (2007) Museum as Artifact, *Toronto Star*, 26 May, p. E1.

Innis, Harold (1951) *The Bias of Communication*. Toronto: University of Toronto Press.

Interpretation Canada website. (n.d.) Accessed 22 June 2019 at https://interpretation canada.wildapricot.org/page-18058.

Iveson, Kurt (1998) Putting the Public Back into Public Space, *Urban Policy and Research*, 16(1), 21–33.

Iveson, Kurt (2007) *Publics and the City*. Malden, MA; Oxford; Carlton, Australia: Blackwell Publishers.

Jagose, Annamarie (2000) Queer World Making: Annamarie Jagose Interviews Michael Warner, *Genders*, 31 [online]. Accessed 27 September 2010 at www.genders.org/g31/g31_jagose.html#n11.

Jameson, Fredric (1991) *Postmodernism, or, The Cultural Logic of Late Capitalism*. Durham, NC: Duke University Press.

Janes, Robert R. (2009) *Museums in a Troubled World: Renewal, Irrelevance or Collapse?* London and New York: Routledge.

Janes, Robert R. (2010). Letter to the Editor, *The Globe and Mail*, 24 August, Section 1, p. 7.

Janes, Robert R. (2015) *Museums without Borders: Selected Writings of Robert R. Janes*. London and New York: Routledge.

Kanngieser, A. (2013) *Experimental Politics and the Making of Worlds*. London: Routledge.

Kelly, Jessica (2008) Courting Public Culture at the ROM, Report, Robarts Centre for Canadian Studies, York University, Toronto.

Kelly, Lynda (2003) Pacific Exhibitions: Front-end Evaluation Results, Australian Museum Audience Research Centre, Sydney.

Kent, Michael L. and Maureen Taylor (2002) Toward a Dialogic Theory of Public Relations, *Public Relations Review*, 28, 21–37.

Kirshenblatt-Gimblett, Barbara (1998) *Destination Culture: Tourism, Museums, and Heritage*. Berkeley, CA: University of California Press.

Knelman, Martin (2009) Museums Entering a Brave New World, *The Toronto Star*, 13 April, p. A13.

Ku, Agnes (2000) Revisiting the Notion of 'Public' in Habermas's Theory – Towards a Theory of Politics of Public Credibility, *Sociological Theory*, 18(2), 216–240.

Ledingham, John A. and Stephen D. Bruning (eds) (2000) *Public Relations as Relationship Management: A Relational Approach to the Study and Practice of Public Relations*. Mahwah, NJ: Lawrence Erlbaum.

Libeskind, Daniel (2001) *The Space of Encounter*. New York: Universe Publications.

Littler, Jo and Roshi Naidoo (eds) (2005) *The Politics of Heritage*. London and New York: Routledge.

Livingstone, Phaedra (2016) Controversy as Catalyst, in Viviane Gosselin and Phaedra Livingstone (eds), *Museums and the Past: Constructing Historical Consciousness*. Vancouver: UBC Press.

Lockett, Christina (1991) Ten Years of Exhibition Evaluation at the Royal Ontario Museum (1980–1990), *ILVS Review: A Journal of Visitor Behavior*, 2(1), 19–47.

Lord, Beth (2007) From the Document to the Monument: Museums and the Philosophy of History, in S. Knell (ed.), *Museum Revolutions* (pp. 355–366). London and New York: Routledge.

Luke, Timothy W. (2002) *Museum Politics: Power Plays at The Exhibition*. Minneapolis, MN: University of Minnesota Press.

Lynch, Bernadette (2014) 'Whose Cake Is It Anyway?': Museums, Civil Society and the Changing Reality of Public Engagement, in Laurence Gouriévidis (ed.), *Museums and Migration: History, Memory and Politics* (pp. 81–94). London and New York: Routledge.

Lynch, Bernadette (2017) The Gate in the Wall: Beyond Happiness-making in Museums, in Bryony Onciul, Michelle L. Stefano, and Stephanie Hawke (eds), *Engaging Heritage, Engaging Communities* (pp. 11–30). Suffolk: Boydell and Brewer.

Lynch, Bernadette and Samuel J.M.M. Alberti (2010) Legacies of Prejudice: Racism, Co-Production and Radical Trust in the Museum, *Museum Management and Curatorship*, 25(1), 13–35.

Macdonald, S. (1996) Theorizing Museums: An Introduction, in Sharon Macdonald and Gordon Fyfe (eds), *Theorizing Museums* (pp. 1–18). Cambridge, MA: Wiley-Blackwell.

MacGregor, Neil (2009) 250 Years On: What Does it Mean to be a World Museum? London: British Museum [Audiofile]. Accessed 3 March 2019 at www.britishmuseum.org/whats_on/events_calendar/recorded_events/250_lecture.aspx.

Mackey, Eva (1995) Postmodernism and Cultural Politics in a Multicultural Nation: Contests over Truth in the Into the Heart of Africa Controversy, *Public Culture*, 7, 403–431.

Mackey, Steve (2006) Misuse of the Term 'Stakeholder' in Public Relations, *PRism* 4(1), 1–15.

Mak, Eileen Diana (1996) Patterns of Change, Sources of Influence: An Historical Study of the Canadian Museum and the Middle Class, 1850–1950, PhD dissertation, University of British Columbia.

Marcus, Julie (2000) Towards an Erotics of the Museum, in Elizabeth Hallam and Brian Street (eds), *Cultural Encounters: Representing 'Otherness'* (pp. 229–244). London and New York: Routledge.

McCarthy, Conal, Jennifer Walklate, Rhiannon Mason, Christopher Whitehead, Jakob Ingemann Parby, André Cicalo, Philipp Schorch, Leslie Witz, Pablo Alonso Gonzalez, Naomi Roux, Eva Ambos, and Ciraj Rassool (2013) Museums in a Global World: A Conversation on Museums, Heritage, Nation, and Diversity in a Transnational Age, *Museum Worlds: Advances in Research*, 1(1), 179–194.

McCracken, Grant (2003) CULTURE and Culture at the Royal Ontario Museum: Anthropology Meets Marketing, Part 2, *Curator*, 46(4), 421–432.

McLean, Fiona (2012) *Marketing the Museum*. London and New York: Routledge.

McLean, Fiona and Mark O'Neill (2007) The 'Social Museum' and its Implication for Marketing, in Ruth Rentschler and Anne-Marie Hede (eds), *Museum Marketing: Competing in the Global Marketplace* (pp. 215–225). Amsterdam: Elsevier.

McTavish, Lianne (2013) *Defining the Modern Museum: A Case Study of the Challenges of Exchange*. Toronto: University of Toronto Press.

Menand, Louis (2009) Professionalization in the Academy, *Harvard Magazine*, November–December. Accessed 24 June 2010 at http://harvardmagazine. com/2009/11/professionalization-in-academy.

Message, Kylie (2006a) The Shock of the Re-newed Modern: MoMA 2004, *Museum and Society*, 4(1), 27–50.

Message, Kylie (2006b) *New Museums and the Making of Culture*. Oxford and New York: Berg.

Message, Kylie (2007) Museums and the Utility of Culture: The Politics of Liberal Democracy and Cultural Well-Being, *Social Identities*, 13(2), 235–256.

Message, Kylie (2009) Museum Studies: Borderwork, Genealogy, Revolution. *Museum and Society*, 7(2), 125–132.

Minkiewicz, Joanna, Jody Evans, and Kerrie Bridson (2014) How Do Consumers Co-Create Their Experiences? An Exploration in the Heritage Sector, *Journal of Marketing Management*, 30(1–2), 30–59.

Morris, Martha (2007) Museum Building Boom or Bust? *Museum Management and Curatorship*, 22(2), 101–108.

Morse, Nuala, Morag Macpherson, and Sophie Robinson (2013) Developing Dialogue in Co-produced Exhibitions: Between Rhetoric, Intentions and Realities, *Museum Management and Curatorship*, 28(1), 91–106.

Mosco, Vincent (1996) The Political Economy of Communication. London: Sage.

Mouffe, Chantal (2000) *The Democratic Paradox*. New York: Verso.

Mullard, Chris (1985) *Race, Power, and Resistance*. London and Boston, MA: Routledge.

Newman, Andrew, F. McLean, and Gordon Urquhart (2005) Museums and the Active Citizen: Tackling the Problems of Social Exclusion, *Citizenship Studies*, 9(1), 41–57.

Newman, Janet and John Clarke (2009) *Publics, Politics and Power: Remaking the Public in Public Services*. London and Thousand Oaks, CA: Sage.

Nora, Pierre (1989) Between Memory and History: Les lieux de mémoire. *Representations*, 26(Spring), 7–24.

Nuttall-Smith, Chris (2008) The Curse of the Aluminum Crystal, *Toronto Life*, September, pp. 55–66.

Nuttall-Smith, Chris (2010) Who Can Save the ROM This Time? *The Globe and Mail*, Friday, 22 January. Accessed 23 January 2010 at www.theglobeandmail.com/news/arts/who-can-save-the-rom-this-time/article1440537/.

Orr, Noreen (2006) Museum Volunteering: Heritage as 'Serious Leisure', *International Journal of Heritage Studies*, 12(2), 194–210.

Parby, Jakob Ingemann (2015) The Theme of Migration as a Tool for Deconstructing and Reconstructing Identities in Museums: Experiences from the Exhibition Becoming a Copenhagener at the Museum of Copenhagen, in Chris Whitehead, Susanna Eckersley *et al.* (eds), *Museums, Migration and Identity in Europe: Peoples, Places and Identities* (pp. 123–148). London: Routledge.

Parker, Martin (2014) University, Ltd: Changing a Business School, *Organization*, 21, 281–292.

Pearson, Ron (1989) A Theory of Public Relations Ethics, unpublished doctoral dissertation, Athens, OH: Ohio University.

Pearson, Ron (1990) Ethical Values or Strategic Values: The Two Faces of Systems Theory in Public Relations, *Public Relations Research Annual*, 2, 219–234.

Peers, Laura and Alison Brown (eds) (2003) *Museums and Source Communities*. London and New York: Routledge.

Phillips, Ruth (2003) Community Collaboration in Exhibitions: Introduction, in Laura Peers and Alison Brown (eds), *Museums and Source Communities* (pp. 155–170). London and New York: Routledge.

Phillips, Ruth (2018) Swings and Roundabouts: Pluralism and the Politics of Change in Canada's National Museums, in Philipp Schorch and Conal McCarthy (eds), *Curatopia: Museums and the Future of Curatorship* (pp. 143–158). Manchester: Manchester University Press.

Procter, Alice (2019) UK Museums Should be Honest about Being Stuffed with Stolen Goods, *Guardian*, 20 February. Accessed 23 February 2019 at www.theguardian.com/commentisfree/2019/feb/20/uk-museums-honest-stolen-goods-imperialism-theft-repatriation.

Rivard, René (1985) Ecomuseums in Quebec, *Museum*, 37(4), 202–205.

Roberts, Lisa C. (1997) *From Knowledge to Narrative: Educators and the Changing Museum*. Washington, DC: Smithsonian Institution Press.

Robertson, K. (2011) Titanium Motherships of the New Economy: Museums, Neoliberalism and Resistance, in Keri Cronin and Kirsty Robertson (eds), *Imagining*

Resistance: Visual Culture and Activism in Canada (pp. 197–214). Waterloo, Canada: Wilfrid Laurier University Press.

Rochon, Lisa (2007) Crystal Scatters No Light, *The Globe and Mail*, Saturday, 2 June.

Roederer, Claire and Marc Filser (2018) Revisiting the Museum Experience, *Qualitative Market Research: An International Journal*, 21(4), 567–587.

ROM (Royal Ontario Museum) (2000) Our Stories Our Future: Strategic Plan, unpublished plan, Toronto: ROM.

ROM (2006) Renaissance ROM Fact Sheet, News Release, January 2006.

ROM (2007a) ICC at the ROM presents Housepaint, Phase 2: Shelter, News Release, 27 November.

ROM (2007b) Department of Museum Volunteers – Celebrating 50 Years [podcast], 18 October.

ROM (2009) Dead Sea Scrolls: Words that Changed the World Opens on 27 June 2009, News Release, 28 April.

ROM (2010) PROM V: Noir, News Release, 24 February.

ROM, Board of Trustees (2010) Board Policy – Public Access. Toronto: Royal Ontario Museum.

Ross, Oakland (2009) Dead Sea Scrolls stir storm at ROM, *The Toronto Star*, 9 April, p. A1.

Ross, Val (2006) Renaissance City: The Billion-dollar Baby, *The Globe and Mail*, Toronto, Saturday, 15 April.

Ruitenbeek, Klaus (2002) Re: Thorsell All-Staff [email correspondence] ROM, 10 July.

Sandell Richard (2007) *Museums, Prejudice and the Reframing of Difference.* London and New York: Routledge.

Sandell, Richard and Robert Janes (2007) *Museum Management and Marketing.* London: Routledge.

Sandell, Richard and Eithne Nightingale (eds) (2012) *Museums, Equality and Social Justice.* London: Routledge.

Schorch, Philipp (2013a) The Experience of a Museum Space, *Museum Management and Curatorship*, 28(2), 193–208.

Schorch, Philipp (2013b) Contact Zones, Third Spaces, and the Act of Interpretation. *Museum and Society*, 11(1), 68–81.

Scott, Carol (2009) Exploring the Evidence Base for Museum Value, *Museum Management and Curatorship*, 24(3), 195–212.

Sharma, Karen (2015) Governing Difficult Knowledge: The Canadian Museum for Human Rights and its Publics, *Review of Education, Pedagogy, and Cultural Studies*, 37(2–3), 184–206.

Shiekh, Simon (2004) Public Spheres and the Function of Progressive Art Institutions, *Republicart*, 2. Accessed 22 June 2019 at www.republicart.net/disc/institution/sheikh01_en.htm.

Shryock, Andrew (ed.) (2004) *Off Stage/On Display: Intimacy and Ethnography in the Age of Public Culture.* Stanford, CA: Stanford University Press.

Silverman, Lois (2009) *The Social Work of Museums.* London and New York: Routledge.

Simon, Nina (2010a) *The Participatory Museum*. Santa Cruz, CA: Museum 2.0.

Simon, Nina (2010b) Museum 2.0: Complicity, Intimacy, Community [online blog] Museum 2.0, 19 May. Accessed 26 June 2019 at http://museumtwo.blog spot.com/2010/05/complicity-intimacy-community.html.

Simon, Roger and Susan Ashley (2010) Introduction: Heritage and Practices of Public Formation, *International Journal of Heritage Studies*, 16(4–5), 247–254.

Smith, Laurajane (2006) *The Uses of Heritage*. London and New York: Routledge.

Splichal, Slavko (2006) In Search of a Strong European Public Sphere: Some Critical Observations on Conceptualizations of Publicness and the (European) Public Sphere, *Media, Culture & Society*, 28(5), 695–714.

Stebbins, Robert A. (1996) Cultural Tourism as Serious Leisure, *Annals of Tourism Research*, 23, 948–950.

Suchy, Sherene (2006) Museum Management: Emotional Value and Community Engagement, INTERCOM 2006 Conference Paper. Accessed 25 August 2010 at www.intercom.museum/documents/3-1Suchy.pdf.

Tator, Carol, Frances Henry, and Winston Matthis (1998) *Challenging Racism in the Arts in Canada: Six Case Studies of Controversy and Conflict.* University of Toronto Press: Toronto.

Teather, J. Lynne (2005) *The Royal Ontario Museum: A Prehistory, 1830–1914.* Toronto and London: Canada University Press.

Thompson, John B. (1995) *The Media and Modernity: A Social Theory of the Media*. Stanford, CA: Stanford University Press.

Thorsell, William (2000) Stay Tuned: The ROM Has a Story to Tell, *The Globe and Mail*, Toronto, Monday, 4 December, pg. R3.

Thorsell, William (2007) The Museum as the New Agora – Notes for an Address to the Empire Club, ROM News Release, 3 May 2007. Accessed 20 August 2009 at www.rom.on.ca/about/pdf/agoraspeech.pdf.

Thorsell, William (2008) Forward, in Kelvin Browne, *Bold Visions: The Architecture of the Royal Ontario Museum*. Toronto: ROM.

Thurlow, Amy (2009) 'I Just Say I'm in Advertising': A Public Relations Identity Crisis? *Canadian Journal of Communication*, 34(2), 245–263.

Tlili, Anwar (2008) Behind the Policy Mantra of the Inclusive Museum: Receptions of Social Exclusion and Inclusion in Museums and Science Centres, *Cultural Sociology*, 2(1), 123–147.

Tolia-Kelly, Divya, Emma Waterton, and Steve Watson (eds) (2016) *Heritage, Affect and Emotion: Politics, Practices and Infrastructures*. London and New York: Routledge.

Tran, Lynn Uyen and Heather King (2007) The Professionalization of Museum Educators: The Case in Science Museums, *Museum Management and Curatorship*, 22(2), 131–149.

Trofanenko, Brenda (ed.) (2014) *Beyond Pedagogy: Reconsidering the Public Purpose of Museums*. Rotterdam: Sense Publishers Springer.

Turney, Michael (1998) Public Relations and Marketing: The Boundaries Blurred and the Functions Blended, North Kentucky University [online]. Accessed 12 January 2019 at www.nku.edu/~turney/prclass/readings/mkting2.html.

Van Krieken, Robert (2012) *Celebrity Society*. London and New York: Routledge.

Vaughan, Kenton, Gordon Henderson, Silva Basmajian, and Colm Feore (2009) *The Museum*, [Documentary film] Toronto: 90th Parallel Film and Television Productions and National Film Board of Canada.

Vergo, Peter (1989) Introduction, in Peter Vergo (ed.), *The New Museology* (pp. 1–5). London: Reaktion Books.

Warner, Michael (2002) Publics and Counterpublics, *Public Culture*, 14(1), 49–90.

Watts, Victoria and Robert W. Gehl (eds) (2010) *The Politics of Cultural Programming in Public Spaces*. Newcastle upon Tyne: Cambridge Scholars Publishing.

Wehmeier, Stefan (2009) Out of the Fog and into the Future: Directions of Public Relations, Theory Building, Research, and Practice, *Canadian Journal of Communication*, 34(2), 265–282.

Weil, Stephen E. (1997) The Museum and the Public, *Museum Management and Curatorship*, 16(3), 257–271.

Weil, Stephen E. (1999) From Being about Something to Being for Somebody: The Ongoing Transformation of the American Museum, *Daedalus*, 128(3), 229–258.

Weinberg, Mark L. and Marsha S. Lewis (2009) The Public Value Approach to Strategic Management, *Museum Management and Curatorship*, 24(3), 253–269.

Weiser, M. Elizabeth (2017) *Museum Rhetoric: Building Civic Identity in National Spaces*. University Park, PA: Penn State Press.

Witcomb, Andrea (2013) Understanding the Role of Affect in Producing a Critical Pedagogy for History Museums, *Museum Management and Curatorship*, 28(3), 255–271.

Whitehead, Christopher (2016) How to Analyze Museum Display: Script, Text, Narrative, CoHERE Critical Archive. Accessed 17 October 2018 at http://digitalcultures.ncl.ac.uk/cohere/wordpress/wp-content/uploads/2016/10/WP1-CAT-1.2.pdf.

Wu, Chin-tao (2002) *Privatising Culture: Corporate Art Intervention Since the 1980s*. London: Verso.

Young, Iris Marion (1990) *Justice and the Politics of Difference*. Princeton, NJ: Princeton University Press.

Zorloni, A. (2010) Managing Performance Indicators in Visual Art Museums, *Museum Management and Curatorship*, 25(2), 167–180.

Documents

Curator X notes, 11 February 2002
Curator X notes, 3 April 2003
DSS Interpretation Plan 2008
DSS minutes, 5 September 2008
DSS minutes, 25 September 2008
DSS minutes, 21 October 2008
DSS minutes, 4 November 2008

DSS minutes, 24 March 2009
DSS minutes, 21 April 2009
Haley Sharpe Communication Strategy 2003
Royal Ontario Museum (2007) Annual Report 2006–2007. Toronto: Royal Ontario Museum.
Royal Ontario Museum (2009) Annual Report 2008–2009. Toronto: Royal Ontario Museum.
Royal Ontario Museum Governors (2009) Spring Newsletter. Toronto: ROM Governors.
ROM Project Brief 2008
ROM Board minutes, 10 December 2009
Thorsell memos to staff: 8 April 2003; 19 February 2009; 7 April; and 26 April 2010

Interviews

Communications coordinator, 5 July 2010
Communications specialist, 12 July 2010
Cultural Agencies, 30 April 2010
Curator A, 3 May 2010
Curator B, 3 May 2010
Curator C, 15 June 2010
DMV president, 6 March 2009
DMV president, 10 May 2010
Education supervisor, 27 April 2010
Education worker, 10 June 2009
Executive assistant, 2 December 2009
Exhibit planner, 20 November 2009
Exhibit planner, 11 December 2009
Expert, 15 April 2010
HR specialist, 5 July 2010
ICC coordinator, 7 June 2010
Marketing coordinator, 4 June 2010
Programming worker, 19 August 2009
Programmes manager, 21 June 2010
Project manager, 13 November 2009
Senior manager, 29 April 2009
Senior manager, 4 March 2009
Senior manager, 27 May 2009
Senior manager, 1 September 2009
Senior manager, 27 November 2009
Staff interviews: 19 August 2009; 27 April 2010; 5 May 2010
Thorsell, 5 November, 11 November, 16 December 2009; Personal email, 17 August 2010
Visitor Relations specialist, 27 November 2009

Visitor Relations specialist, 20 May 2010
Visitor interviews: 1 December, 15 December, 14 December, 22 December 2009;
   1 May 2010
Volunteer 1, 23 April 2009
Volunteer 2, 27 April 2009
Volunteer 3, 4 May 2009
Volunteer 4, 9 May 2009
Volunteer 5, 22 October 2009
Volunteer 6, 6 May 2009
Volunteer 7, 27 May 2009

Index

For Product Safety Concerns and Information please contact our EU
representative GPSR@taylorandfrancis.com
Taylor & Francis Verlag GmbH, Kaufingerstraße 24, 80331 München, Germany